Beauty by The Book *for Teens*

Becoming a Biblically Beautiful Young Woman
A 7-Week Study of Proverbs

Laurie Cole
Author & Teacher

Production Coordinator • Pam Henderson
Cover and Layout Design • Debbie Todd
Graphic Design • Julie Riley, j.riley creative LLC
Editorial Team • Emily Ryan and Hannah Mahanay
Photography • Don & Mary Carico, Lakewood Photography, League City, TX

Priority Ministries

Encouraging Women to Give God Glory & Priority

www.priorityministries.org

Dedication

To Juliette,
my precious granddaughter.
I love you to pieces.

Acknowledgements

Priority Ministries was privileged and blessed to pilot *Beauty by The Book for Teens* in 2010 with a fantastic group of teenage girls from **Sagemont Church in Houston, Texas**, and their leaders, **Scott Condict**, Minister to Students, and **Ruth Birdsong**, Minister to Girls.

Each week of the pilot, the girls completed their *Beauty by The Book for Teens* homework, participated in small groups, and met with Laurie for a teaching session. And each and every week, they graciously and patiently filled out evaluation forms providing us with invaluable insights which enabled us to revise and improve the study you now hold in your hands. We thank the Lord for each and every girl who participated in the pilot, for their leaders, and for the tremendous blessing they've been to us and, ultimately, to you.

We also want to recognize and express our love and gratitude to **Wanda Shellenbarger**, Women's and Girl's Ministry Director, First Baptist Church Carl Junction, Missouri, whose encouragement, example, and prayer support was absolutely key in the development of *Beauty by The Book for Teens*. Thank you, Wanda, for your heart to reach and teach God's Word to teenage girls. We are especially grateful for your love for the girls in the Missouri Baptist Children's Homes. God used your example and the precious testimonies of the girls you taught there to inspire us to step out by faith and produce *Beauty by The Book for Teens*, our very first Bible study for girls.

"I thank my God in all my remembrance of you."
Philippians 1:3 *NAS*

About the Study

This Bible study is a simple tool to help you discover life-changing truths from God's Word. Think of this workbook as a chisel and your Bible as a gold mine. Each day you'll "dig-in" to God's Word to discover precious treasures that will enrich your life for His glory (Psalm 19:9–10, 119:162). Homework for this study will require approximately 20 minutes per day, five days per week.

The Holy Spirit will be your Divine Tutor throughout this study (John 16:13), and prayer will be essential in facilitating your sensitivity to His leadership. Therefore, a *pray* paragraph is included at the beginning of each day's homework. At the conclusion of your daily study, you'll be encouraged to record any insights the Holy Spirit has shown you in a brief *reflect* section.

A good translation of the Bible will be essential as you use this study. The *New Living Translation*, Second Edition, the *New International Version*, the *New American Standard Bible*, the *New King James Version*, or the *King James Version* are all very accurate translations and are highly recommended. In this study, the author will primarily use the *New Living Translation*.

Also included in this workbook are seven Listening Guides. These fill-in-the-blank guides are designed to be used with the *Beauty by The Book for Teens* downloadable videos, DVD or CD sets which include seven teaching sessions with Laurie Cole (approximately 25–30 minutes per session). The *Beauty by The Book for Teens* downloadable videos, DVD or CD sets are recommended but are optional. For more information about these resources, please visit www.priorityministries.com/shop.

About the Author

Laurie Cole is the Founder and President of Priority Ministries, a ministry dedicated to encouraging and equipping women to love God most and seek Him first. Raised in a strong Christian home, Laurie became a Christian at an early age. But in her early twenties, God tested and taught her the importance of truly giving Him priority in her life.

In 1985, Laurie enrolled in an in-depth women's Bible study. Encouraged by the older women who led the study, Laurie received training and began teaching and leading a group where God affirmed His call upon her life to teach. For over 20 years, Laurie has taught dozens of Bible studies, spoken at numerous women's events and conferences, and is the author of three in-depth Bible studies: *There Is A Season*, *The Temple*, and *Beauty by The Book*. Her passion for God and hunger for His Word continues to grow.

A minister's wife, Laurie and her husband, Bill, serve the Lord at Sagemont Church in Houston, Texas, where he is the Associate Pastor of Worship and Praise. They have been married for 32 years and have three sons (David, Kevin, and J.J.), one beloved daughter-in-law (Stephanie), and two glorious grandchildren (Ezra and Juliette).

Table of Contents

Introduction to the Study

I am absolutely overjoyed that you are holding this book in your hands! You see, I never intended to write a Bible study specifically targeted at teens, but God had other plans—and those plans included you. Let me explain.

A few years ago, I wrote and released *Beauty by The Book* for the same group of women I've pretty much always written for and taught: adult women. Women 21 and older. But right after those women started doing the study, something very unexpected happened. Those women began asking me about you. They'd say things like:

"This study has taught me how to become a godly woman.
Now I can't wait to teach it to my girls small group.
Do you have a Beauty by The Book *workbook just for teens?"*

"I can't wait to do this study with my teen-age daughter.
I want her to learn these truths while she's young. I sure wish I had."

"My life would have been radically different if someone had taught me
these principles when I was a teenager. I hope one day you'll write a
Beauty by The Book Bible *study for young women. They really need it."*

My response to women who told me things like that was always, "Thanks for the encouragement. I'll pray about it." So I did. I prayed, and prayed, and prayed, until God showed me very clearly that you had always been part of His plan for this study. What a delightful surprise that was to me!

But there's another reason why writing this study for you is such a surprise to me. As the mother of three sons, I have never enjoyed the privilege of raising girls or of teaching a daughter how to become a godly woman—and I didn't think I ever would. But God always knew about you. What a gift it is to study and share His Word with you, precious you.

In today's culture, beauty is an idol worshipped and pursued by multitudes of women both young and old. Biblical beauty, however, is vastly different from worldly beauty—but you probably already know that. What you may not know, however, is just how much you have been influenced by the world's definition and beliefs about beauty. Therefore, before you even begin this study, I must warn you: Pursuing biblical beauty will require you to swim against some very strong cultural currents. But you can do it!

Like the constantly changing hemlines of today's fashions, the world's definition of beauty will continually evolve. But one thing will never change: God's Word—The Book. More relevant today than the latest issue of *Seventeen*. More liberating than the most recent reinvention of feminism. God's Word is timeless, transformational, and true. Study its standards, practice its principles and you will become a true beauty—a biblically beautiful young woman of God.

Your Sister,

Laurie

> *"The grass withers, and the flowers fade,*
> *but the Word of our God stands forever."*
> —Isaiah 40:8 *NLT*

Introductory Week • *Physical Beauty vs. Biblical Beauty*

Physical Beauty...

1) Is _____-_____. *Ezekiel 28:12*

2) Is _____-_____. *Ezekiel 28:13–14*

3) Is _____-_____. *Ezekiel 28:17*

4) Is _____ _____. *Ezekiel 28:16–17*

Biblical Beauty...

1) Is _____-_____. *1 Peter 3:4*

2) Is _____ and _____. *1 Peter 3:4*

3) Is _____ in God's sight. *1 Peter 3:4*

4) Is _____ and _____. *1 Peter 3:4*

Question: How can you become a biblically beautiful young woman?

Answer: By _____ God and _____
the standard of His Word.

Week 1 • *Five Beauty Dos & Don'ts*

This week, I will be introducing you to five women. These five females all make their home in the Book of Proverbs. For the next six weeks, we will be spending quite a bit of time with them as we learn how to become biblically beautiful. But before you meet them, you need to know something: not all of these women qualify as true biblical beauties.

Let me explain. You've probably seen those "beauty do" and "beauty don't" photos in the fashion magazines haven't you? Well, some of the five women you're about to meet are biblical "beauty dos," but others are biblical "beauty don'ts." And trust me, you won't have any trouble telling which ones are which.

So, c'mon. Let's head to Proverbs—our home for the next six weeks.

Day One

I almost forgot to tell you, there is a sixth "woman" we'll be getting to know in Proverbs. Her name is Wisdom. All throughout Proverbs, the author uses the female pronoun "she" to refer to wisdom. Don't you just love that! But let's not get too carried away, because there is a seventh "woman" mentioned in the Proverbs, and her name is Folly.

This sixth "woman"—Wisdom—will be the focus of our daily *pray* time. If you want to become a biblically beautiful young woman, it is essential that you get to know Ms. Wisdom well.

pray

1. Good news! Wisdom is available to everyone who needs it, and we *all* need it. James 1:5 promises that "if any of you lack wisdom, let him ask of God who gives to all men generously and without reproach and it will be given to him" (*NASB*). Begin your first day of study by bowing your head and praising God as the source of true wisdom. Ask Him to pour out His wisdom upon you and make you wise.

> *Wisdom shouts in the streets.*
> *She cries out in the public square…*
> *"Come here and listen to me!*
> *I'll pour out the spirit of wisdom*
> *upon you and make you wise."*
> —Proverbs 1:20–23

2. Brace yourself. You're about to meet Beauty #1, the first female mentioned in Proverbs, and she's a doozy. Allow me to introduce you to the **Immoral Woman** as you read Proverbs 5:3–6:

> ³ *For the lips of an adulteress [woman] drip honey,*
> *and her speech is smoother than oil;*
> ⁴ *but in the end she is bitter as gall,*
> *sharp as a double edged sword.*
> ⁵ *Her feet go down to death;*
> *her steps lead straight to the grave.*
> ⁶ *She gives no thought to the way of life;*
> *her paths are crooked, but she knows it not.*
> —Proverbs 5:3–6 *NIV*

3. Based upon Proverbs 5:3–6, please answer the following questions about the Immoral Woman:

    a. What's the very first thing you learned about her, and what kind of first impression does she usually make (verse 3)?

    b. According to verse 4, what will others eventually discover about her, and when will they discover it?

    c. What is her final destination and why (verses 5–6)?

    You've just experienced your first encounter with the Immoral Woman, but it won't be your last. Next week, you'll study her extensively, and you may be surprised to learn that five passages and one entire chapter of Proverbs are devoted to her. She gets more press and attention than any of the other four women we'll be studying, and she certainly gets the most press in today's world, which leads me to ask this:

4. If you had to name the top three places you most consistently see the Immoral Woman in our culture, where would they be? For example: on television.

5. Why do you think five passages and one entire chapter of Proverbs are devoted to the Immoral Woman? In other words, why would God want us to get to know her so well?

6. A few minutes ago, you prayed and asked God for wisdom. What wisdom has He given you through your study today?

reflect

Day Two

pray

1. Tuning into God has never been more difficult than it is today. Hearing His still, small voice over the nonstop noise of technology—ringing cell phones, texting alerts, and 24/7 access to the internet—is no small feat. But by daily and deliberately making today's Proverb a priority, you can still hear God speak. So, right now, tune out the racket around you, and tune in to God and His wisdom through prayer.

> *Tune your ears to wisdom, and*
> *concentrate on understanding.*
>
> —Proverbs 2:2

Today you will meet two more women from Proverbs: the Indiscreet Woman and the Irritating Woman. I know. They probably don't sound like the kind of women who can teach us much about biblical beauty, but here's a great passage to remind us why we can't afford to ignore them:

*All Scripture is inspired by God and is useful to teach us what is true
and to make us realize what is wrong in our lives. It straightens us out
and teaches us to do what is right. It is God's way of preparing us in every way,
fully equipped for every good thing God wants us to do.*
—2 Timothy 3:16–17

2. Keeping 2 Timothy 3:16–17 in mind, meet Beauty #2 by reading the following scripture:

*A woman who is beautiful but lacks discretion
is like a gold ring in a pig's snout.*
— Proverbs 11:22

Wow! That's one blunt verse, huh? While Beauty #2, the **Indiscreet Woman**, may be rich in the looks department, her lack of discretion is her ruin. Thus, one of the primary principles we can learn from her is that no amount of make-up, spa treatments, Botox® injections, or even plastic surgery can cover up a deficit of discretion.

So what exactly is discretion? To answer that question, find and circle the synonyms of discretion hidden in the Word Search puzzle.

Synonyms of Discretion

```
S  F  U  S  U  I  A  L  B  S  J  N  Y  P  G  N  I
B  N  N  R  V  X  W  U  Y  S  E  I  K  X  J  O  O
F  O  D  K  G  R  B  I  B  G  X  J  X  O  H  I  E
J  S  E  L  O  C  D  I  S  C  E  R  N  M  E  N  T
I  U  R  J  O  K  V  S  F  D  M  O  O  K  Z  U  K
Z  F  S  A  D  U  N  P  X  P  O  D  X  K  T  B  K
V  F  T  U  T  E  W  E  B  N  H  M  P  J  R  E  N
L  K  A  M  A  S  E  R  Y  G  D  U  D  E  F  S  O
G  C  N  L  S  B  K  H  G  C  P  H  N  P  Z  V  W
O  F  D  U  T  S  S  E  L  F  C  O  N  T  R  O  L
O  N  I  W  E  T  M  D  C  C  N  C  L  F  B  U  E
D  S  N  K  Q  T  A  C  P  S  C  E  E  F  R  Z  D
S  D  G  O  O  D  J  U  D  G  M  E  N  T  J  U  G
E  C  L  F  B  F  U  S  K  I  R  Q  T  A  C  T  E
N  C  E  E  F  R  Z  D  Q  M  R  J  B  A  H  Y  L
S  S  C  L  I  N  T  E  L  L  I  G  E  N  C  E  A
E  O  J  L  H  T  R  A  F  Y  Z  Z  X  T  K  B  C
```

Wisdom	Discernment	Understanding
Knowledge	Intelligence	Self-control
Good judgment	Good sense	Good taste

3. After seeing those synonyms, it's pretty obvious, huh? Discretion is a must-have for every biblically beautiful young woman. In a couple of weeks, we'll study discretion in detail. But for now, discover how you can get discretion by picking up your Bible, reading Proverbs 1:1–5, and answering the following questions:

    a. Who wrote the Book of Proverbs?

    b. Why did he write it (verses 2–5)?

    c. According to this passage, how can we obtain discretion?

OK, let's move along now and meet Beauty #3, the **Irritating Woman**. We're not going to spend much time with her today, but that's OK. A little time with her goes a long way!

4. Meet Beauty #3 by reading the following scriptures:

    NOTE: The word "contentious" means argumentative and quarrelsome.[1]

    > *It is better to live alone in the corner of an attic*
    > *than with a contentious wife in a lovely home.*
    > —Proverbs 21:9

    > *It is better to live alone in the desert*
    > *than with a crabby complaining wife.*
    > — Proverbs 21:19

    We've all met women like this before haven't we? But let's be honest: at times, we've all been her, too. And while these verses may apply to women, you and I both know that crabbiness does not discriminate. Anyone (young or old, male or female, single or married, Christian or non-Christian) can exhibit the classic symptoms of what I call "3C Syndrome": (1) Contentiousness, (2) Crabbiness, with frequent bouts of (3) Complaining.

    Fortunately, 3C is not generally contagious, and there is a cure (we'll uncover it in the weeks ahead). But for now, let's focus on the primary and possible long-term effects of 3C.

5. According to Proverbs 21:9 and 19:

    a. How does 3C affect our relationships with others?

    b. What potential long-term effects could 3C cause in our relationships with others?

6. Might *you* have a mild (or possibly serious) case of 3C? Take a quick check-up by circling the word that most accurately completes each of the following sentences:

   a. My friends and family would probably say that I am crabby:
      rarely   occasionally   frequently

   b. My friends and family would probably say that I complain:
      rarely   occasionally   frequently

   c. My friends and family would probably say that I am usually:
      easygoing   a little high-maintenance   downright difficult

   d. My friends and family would probably say that my words are usually:
      encouraging and kind   sweet and sour   negative and nagging

7. If your check-up revealed a possible case of 3C, a quick dose of wisdom and instruction from Proverbs should ease some of your symptoms until we can study the cure in the weeks ahead. Begin applying the following verses to your life as often and as liberally as needed:

   Don't talk too much, for it fosters sin.
   Be sensible and turn off the flow!
   —Proverbs 10:19

   Kind words are like honey—
   Sweet to the soul and healthy for the body.
   —Proverbs 16:24

8. Do you agree that there is a lot we can learn from the two women we've met today? What insights has the Holy Spirit taught you today through the Indiscreet Woman and the Irritating Woman?

reflect

_____

_____

_____

_____

Day Three

pray

1. The fear of the Lord is a very positive and beneficial thing. It is where true wisdom begins. So what exactly is it? Very simply, the fear of the Lord is reverence (deep respect and awe[2]) for God that results in obedience to God. It is both attitude (reverence) and action (obedience); and when you put them together, you get wisdom! Before you begin today's study, submit yourself in reverence before God in prayer, and commit to obey Him. Then watch for wisdom to show up.

*Fear of the LORD
is the beginning of wisdom.
Knowledge of the Holy One
results in understanding.*
—Proverbs 9:10

2. I am very excited today to introduce you to Beauty #4. This woman bears no resemblance to the three women you have previously met in Proverbs—thank goodness! So, without further adieu, it is my privilege to introduce you now to Beauty #4, the **Captivating Woman**:

> [18] *Let your wife be a fountain of blessing for you.*
> *Rejoice in the wife of your youth.*
> [19] *She is a loving doe, a graceful deer.*
> *Let her breasts satisfy you always.*
> *May you always be captivated by her love.*
> —Proverbs 5:18–19

Every scripture in the Bible is inspired by God. He is the ultimate Author of every passage and verse (2 Peter 1:21). Therefore, when you read a sensual passage like Proverbs 5:18–19, you need to remember that God Himself wrote it. So it's pretty obvious to see that when it comes to sex, God is no prude. But to more fully understand God's view about sex, you need to take a second look at Proverbs 5:18–19.

3. Circle the correct answer to each of the following questions:

    a. According to Proverbs 5:18–19, who is God encouraging to enjoy sex?

    Any man   A husband

    b. According to Proverbs 5:18–19, who is the captivating woman?

    Any woman   A wife

    a. According to Proverbs 5:18–19, who is God instructing and encouraging to enjoy sexual intimacy?

    Any relationship   A married couple

The first seven chapters of Proverbs are specifically addressed from a father (Solomon, the author of Proverbs) to his son. In Proverbs 5:18–19, the father is exhorting his son to seek love and sexual satisfaction within the bounds of a monogamous marriage to a Captivating Woman.

But Proverbs 5:18–19 has a message for women, too. I believe it teaches women—married women—to be sensually, sexually satisfying wives. So as an unmarried teenager, how does this passage apply to you? I believe God's message to you is this: When you become a wife, you should become a Captivating Woman…but not until then.

4. From the beginning, God designed and reserved sex for marriage. See it for yourself by opening your Bible and reading Genesis 2:21–25. It's the beautiful account of the very first bride and the very first wedding (and note in verse 22 who gives the bride away—so amazing!). After you've read this passage, write out verses 24–25 word-for-word.

5. How does Genesis 2:21-25 parallel Proverbs 5:18–19?

6. Describe the conflict you see between our culture's view of sex and the biblical view of sex.

7. As a young woman, how has God spoken to your heart through His Word today?

Day Four

pray

{

1. What's at the top of your "want list"? You know what I mean—most of us have a list in our head of things we'd really like to have. But do you know what should always be at the very top? Wisdom. Take today's passage before the Lord in prayer, and commit to giving it priority on your "want list."

> *Choose (wisdom's) instruction rather than silver,*
> *and knowledge over pure gold.*
> *For wisdom is far more valuable than rubies.*
> *Nothing you desire can be compared with it.*
> —Proverbs 8:10–11

2. Thus far, you've met the first four women from Proverbs. Are you ready to meet our final beauty, Beauty #5? You may have heard about her before. Hands down, she's the most well-known woman in Proverbs. Prepare to be dazzled as you meet Beauty #5: the **Ideal Woman**.

Proverbs 31:10–31

¹⁰ *Who can find a virtuous and capable wife? She is worth more than precious rubies.*

¹¹ *Her husband can trust her, and she will greatly enrich his life.*

¹² *She will not hinder him but help him all her life.*

¹³ *She finds wool and flax and busily spins it.*

¹⁴ *She is like a merchant's ship; she brings her food from afar.*

¹⁵ *She gets up before dawn to prepare breakfast for her household and plan the day's work for her servant girls.*

¹⁶ *She goes out to inspect a field and buys it; with her earnings she plants a vineyard.*

¹⁷ *She is energetic and strong, a hard worker.*

¹⁸ *She watches for bargains; her lights burn late into the night.*

¹⁹ *Her hands are busy spinning thread, her fingers twisting fiber.*

²⁰ *She extends a helping hand to the poor and opens her arms to the needy.*

²¹ *She has no fear of winter for her household because all of them have warm clothes.*

²² *She quilts her own bedspreads. She dresses like royalty in gowns of finest cloth.*

²³ *Her husband is well known, for he sits in the council meeting with the other civic leaders.*

²⁴ She makes belted linen garments and sashes to sell to the merchants.

²⁵ She is clothed with strength and dignity, and she laughs with no fear of the future.

²⁶ When she speaks, her words are wise, and kindness is the rule when she gives instructions.

²⁷ She carefully watches all that goes on in her household and does not have to bear the consequences of laziness.

²⁸ Her children stand and bless her. Her husband praises her:

²⁹ "There are many virtuous and capable women in the world, but you surpass them all!"

³⁰ Charm is deceptive, and beauty does not last; but a woman who fears the LORD will be greatly praised.

³¹ Reward her for all she has done. Let her deeds publicly declare her praise.

After reading such an extensive passage extolling the virtues of the Ideal Woman, the phrase "total package" comes to my mind. Wow! This woman's got it all and, furthermore, she's got it all *very* together.

But don't get the idea that this passage is describing a typical day-in-the-life-of the Ideal Woman. No one can do everything mentioned in this passage in a single day. Instead, Proverbs 31:10-31 paints a panoramic picture for us of the Ideal Women's life, character, and career as a wife, mother, entrepreneur, and servant of God. Here we see samples of the seasons of a woman's life. But we also see something else: a role model for women young and old.

3. As you read Proverbs 31:10–31, which of the Ideal Woman's qualities, characteristics, and accomplishments do you most desire for your own life?

4. Prepare today to become an Ideal Woman someday. Find out how by reading 1 Timothy 4:12, underlining it in your Bible, and writing it out word-for-word below.

5. How has God spoken to your heart through His Word today?

reflect

_____

_____

_____

_____

Day Five

pray

1. The Book of Proverbs is a collection of wise sayings written and edited by Solomon to teach us how to live wise, godly lives (Proverbs 1:1–6). The benefits of wise living are obvious in the following Proverb. As you conclude the first week of your study, pray and thank God for the wisdom you've already gleaned and for the benefits you've already seen.

*Wisdom
will multiply your days
and add years to your life.
If you become **wise**,
you will be the one to benefit.
If you scorn **wisdom**,
you will be the one to suffer.*
—Proverbs 9:11–12

This week, you've briefly met the five females from Proverbs. In the next five weeks, these women will teach us the basics of biblical beauty. But before we conclude this first week of study, there's one very important thing we must do: we need to define biblical beauty.

The first thing you need to know is that biblical beauty is very different from physical beauty, the kind of beauty our world worships. Every single day, girls are bombarded with images of the world's definition of beauty: perfect hair, perfect clothes and (above all) the perfect shape, size, and weight. The result? Millions of girls strive to attain that standard, and many of them end up struggling with poor self-image, eating disorders, depression, and other forms of self-destructive behavior.

But is the world's definition of beauty true? To answer that question, you need to go to the very source of truth: God's Word. In fact, Jesus affirmed that God's Word is true ("Thy word is truth." John 17:17). So, pick up your copy of The Truth—your Bible—and begin your final day of study this week as you discover the real truth about beauty and how God defines it.

2. According to the following passages, what do you learn about biblical beauty? Record your answers in the space provided.

   a. 1 Samuel 16:7

   b. 1 Peter 3:3–4

3. The prophet Isaiah foretold Christ's coming in great detail. He even provided us with information about Jesus' physical appearance and beauty. Read Isaiah 53:2, and record what you learn about the beauty of Christ.

   NOTE: the "He" in this verse refers to Christ.

4. Using all of the scriptural information you acquired in Questions 2 and 3, define biblical beauty in your own words by completing the following sentence:

   Biblical beauty is…

5. Based upon everything you've studied this week about biblical beauty, check the box that correctly describes each of our 5 Beauties from the Proverbs:

   a. The Immoral Woman is a: ❑ Biblical Beauty Do
   ❑ Biblical Beauty Don't

   b. The Indiscreet Woman is a: ❑ Biblical Beauty Do
   ❑ Biblical Beauty Don't

   c. The Irritating Woman is a: ❑ Biblical Beauty Do
   ❑ Biblical Beauty Don't

   d. The Captivating Woman is a: ❑ Biblical Beauty Do
   ❑ Biblical Beauty Don't

   e. The Ideal Woman is a: ❑ Biblical Beauty Do
   ❑ Biblical Beauty Don't

6. Be honest. Be real. How has the world's definition of beauty affected you?

7. Now, think about this: How will pursuing biblical beauty affect you?

8. It's time to make a choice, precious girl. What kind of beauty will you choose to pursue? Please circle one:

    Physical Beauty   Biblical Beauty

9. You've had a great week of study. You've saturated your heart with God's Word, and you've given Him an opportunity to speak truth into your life. So, as you reflect upon all that you've learned and studied, what has the Lord most impressed upon your heart and life?

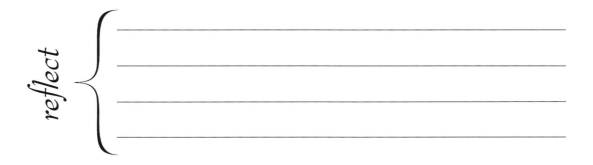

On June 14, 2007, a well-known biblical beauty died. After many years of declining health, Ruth Bell Graham (wife of evangelist Billy Graham) went to be with the Lord at the age of 87. At her funeral, her children remembered her as funny, feisty, and full of love for Jesus and His Word.

Although he was not expected nor scheduled to speak, Billy Graham rose spontaneously to his feet and spoke at Ruth's service. In his brief address, he recalled the previous evening when he'd visited the funeral home to see Ruth one last time. Then he said, "I wish you could look into the casket because she's so beautiful." Ruth's beauty transcended even death.

In a world that worships physical, temporal beauty, the life and death of Ruth Bell Graham proves that biblical beauty is timeless and eternal. It has the awesome power to grow and intensify even as our bodies weaken and fade. It is the amazing promise to all who love the Lord and live His Word. It is real beauty. It is rare beauty. It is beauty by The Book.

NOTE: Find out more about Ruth Graham's childhood, teen-age, and adult life by reading her biography, *Ruth: A Portrait, The Story of Ruth Bell Graham*, by Patricia Cornwell. You'll love it!

Week One • *Biblical Beauty According to Proverbs*

Background on Proverbs:

1) *Author of Proverbs:* _____ Proverbs 1:1

2) *Purpose of Proverbs* (1:2–6): To give wisdom, discipline, understanding, prudence, knowledge and discretion to the _____ AND the _____.

3) *Primary Principle of Proverbs* (1:7): The fear of the Lord is the _____/_____ of wisdom and knowledge.

   The fear of the Lord = _____ for God

   that results in _____ to God.

4) *Present Day Proverb:*

   "_____."

   Our Goal as we study Proverbs: To _____ **AND**

   _____/_____ **God better.**

Biblical Beauty Dos: According to Proverbs:

1) _____ and _____. (Beauty Don't #1: The Immoral Woman)

2) _____ and _____. (Beauty Don't #2: The Indiscreet Woman)

3) _____ and _____. (Beauty Don't #3: The Irritating Woman)

4) _____ and _____. (Beauty Do #1: The Captivating Woman)

5) _____ and _____. (Beauty Do #2: The Ideal Woman)

Week 2 • *The Immoral Woman*

Teen hotties. Visit any mall in America and you'll spot them sporting skintight t-shirts and jeans, baring their cleavage proudly, and shopping for lingerie with their boyfriends in Victoria's Secret. As far as the culture is concerned, none of this is a big deal. But what about God? Is He concerned about teen hotties? Absolutely, but it might surprise you to know that He's not one bit shocked by them either.

So who is this hottie our culture craves and adores? The Bible calls her the Immoral Woman and guess what? She wants you to become her friend…and her follower. But beware, because this is where her friendship will ultimately lead you: "The lips of an immoral woman are as sweet as honey…[but] her steps lead straight to the grave" (Proverbs 5:3–5). Make no mistake, the Immoral Woman is a sweet-talking, back-stabbing, satanic strategist, and she's hell-bent on one thing: destroying you.

Girl, it's time to rise up and declare war on the Immoral Woman. But there's only one way to defeat her: you must arm yourself with the truth of God's Word—it's kryptonite to every satanic power including her. So study well this week, because victory is yours for the taking.

> *You are from God, little children, and have overcome them;*
> *because greater is He who is in you than he who is in the world.*
> —1 John 4:4 *NASB*

Day One

1. Begin your study this week in prayer by asking God to search your heart and reveal all the impurities in your life. Be still. Allow God to speak to you. Take time to confess each sin to Him, and receive His cleansing and forgiveness. Commit to complete repentance, and ask God for wisdom to keep you pure.

> *Wisdom will save you from the immoral woman,*
> *from the flattery of the adulterous woman.*
> —Proverbs 2:16

The Immoral Woman has become so popular these days that some people don't even recognize her for the heartbreaking, troublemaking seductress that she is. I'm telling you, this gal is dangerous! That's why this week we're going to shine the light of God's Word directly on her and expose her for who she really is.

But there's another reason we need to take a long, hard, scriptural look at the Immoral Woman: **we must make sure that our lives bear no resemblance whatsoever to hers.**

2. Read Proverbs 2:16–19, then answer the following questions:

> *16 Wisdom will save you from the immoral woman,*
> *from the seductive words of the promiscuous woman.*
> *17 She has abandoned her husband*
> *and ignores the covenant she made before God.*
> *18 Entering her house leads to death;*
> *it is the road to the grave.*
> *19 The man who visits her is doomed.*
> *He will never reach the paths of life.*
> —Proverbs 2:16–19

a. In the first line of verse 16, this woman is called "the immoral woman." What is she called in the second line of verse 16, and what does this mean? If you're uncertain, please look for the definition in a dictionary or online at <u>Dictionary.com</u>.

b. How does she speak (v. 16)?

c. How does she treat God and others (v. 17)?

d. How dangerous is she?

3. Another description of the Immoral Woman is found in Proverbs 5:3–6. As you read it, circle the words and phrases that are similar to the Proverbs 2:16–19 description

> *³ The lips of an immoral woman are as sweet as honey,*
> *and her mouth is smoother than oil.*
> *⁴ but the result is bitter as poison,*
> *sharp as a double-edged sword.*
> *⁵ Her feet go down to death;*
> *her steps lead straight to the grave.*
> *⁶ She does not care about the path to life.*
> *She staggers down a crooked trail and*
> *doesn't even realize where it leads.*
> —Proverbs 5:3–6

4. Proverbs 30:20 reveals, perhaps, the most dangerous aspect of the Immoral Woman's attitude and character. Part of this verse (from the *NLT*) is recorded for you. Use your Bible to record the shocking final words of this verse (an actual quote from the Immoral Woman herself) in the blank provided.

NOTE: If your Bible translation is hard for you to understand, go online to www.biblegateway.com and read Proverbs 30:20 from another Bible translation such as the New Living Translation, New International Version, or the New American Standard.

An adulterous woman consumes a man, then wipes her mouth and says,

"_____"

—Proverbs 30:20

5. I want you to really think about the quote you just read spoken straight from the lips of the Immoral Woman. Examine her words in Proverbs 30:20, and discover why she's so dangerous by answering the following questions:

   a. What do the Immoral Woman's words reveal about her character and her sense of right and wrong?

   b. What do the Immoral Woman's words reveal about her concern for the guys she seduces and others who may be hurt by her actions?

   c. As you consider your answers to the previous two questions, why is the Immoral Woman so dangerous to others?

6. What insights has the Holy Spirit given you through your study today? How can you use what you've learned?

reflect

Day Two

1. As you begin today's study in prayer, acknowledge your need for wisdom before God. Tell Him that you recognize He is your source for wisdom, and ask Him to speak to you through the pages of His Word.

   For the Lord grants wisdom!
   From his mouth come knowledge and understanding.
   —Proverbs 2:6

ights, camera, action! The passage you're about to read is written so vividly that it's almost like watching a movie. It is the longest, most descriptive passage ever written about the Immoral Woman in the Scriptures, and it sheds more light on her ways and wiles than any of the passages you studied yesterday. Get ready for an Academy Award-winning performance by a woman playing her part to perfection, our Beauty Don't #1, the **Immoral Woman**.

2. Your primary assignment today is to read and examine Proverbs 7:4–27 and to:

   • Circle any words or phrases used to describe the Immoral Woman's negative character qualities, speech, behavior, and heart.

   • Make notes of your own observations about her and the way she operates in the margins beside this passage.

   To help you get started, I've already circled a couple of words, and you'll also see one of my notes in the margin. I encourage you to fill up the margins with your insights and personal "takes" on the Immoral Woman. The margins of my own copy of this passage are full of notes I've taken and I have to tell you, there's something very empowering about exposing this gal for who she really is.

Proverbs 7:4-27

⁴ *Love wisdom like a sister; make insight a beloved member of your family.*

⁵ *Let them hold you back from an affair with an immoral woman, from listening to the ⟨flattery⟩ of an adulterous woman.*

⁶ *I was looking out the window of my house one day*

⁷ *and saw a simpleminded young man who lacked common sense.*

⁸ *He was crossing the street near the house of an immoral woman. He was strolling down the path by her house*

⁹ *at twilight, as the day was fading, as the dark of night set in.*

¹⁰ *The woman approached him, ⟨dressed seductively⟩ and sly of heart.*

¹¹ *She was the brash, rebellious type who never stays at home.*

¹² *She is often seen in the streets and markets, soliciting at every corner.*

¹³ *She threw her arms around him and kissed him, and with a brazen look she said,*

¹⁴ *"I've offered my sacrifices and just finished my vows.*

¹⁵ *It's you I was looking for! I came out to find you, and here you are!*

¹⁶ *My bed is spread with colored sheets of finest linen imported from Egypt.*

¹⁷ *I've perfumed my bed with myrrh, aloes, and cinnamon.*

¹⁸ *Come, let's drink our fill of love until morning. Let's enjoy each other's caresses,*

¹⁹ *for my husband is not home. He's away on a long trip.*

²⁰ *He has taken a wallet full of money with him, and he won't return until later in the month."*

²¹ *So she seduced him with her pretty speech. With her flattery she enticed him.*

²² *He followed her at once, like an ox going to the slaughter or like a trapped stag,*

²³ *awaiting the arrow that would pierce its heart. He was like a bird flying into a snare, little knowing it would cost him his life.*

²⁴ *Listen to me, my sons, and pay attention to my words.*

²⁵ *Don't let your hearts stray away toward her. Don't wander down her wayward path.*

²⁶ *For she has been the ruin of many; numerous men have been her victims.*

²⁷ *Her house is the road to the grave. Her bedroom is the den of death.*

She makes the first move; she's one aggressive chick.

Proverbs 7:10 tells us that the Immoral Woman dresses "seductively" which means she dresses with the intent to entice her prey. Her body is her bait, and she makes sure her clothes leave very little to a guy's imagination.

Many teens today are dressing just like the Immoral Woman…and sadly, some of them are Christians. Nancy Leigh DeMoss, a Christian author and teacher (www.reviveourhearts.com), has a wonderful message entitled *Does God Really Care What I Wear*? I love the question in that title. Let's find the answer together right now.

3. Read 1 Timothy 2:9–10 and 1 Peter 3:3–4 and record what you learn about God's dress code for women.

4. Based upon what you've learned today from Proverbs, 1 Timothy, and 1 Peter:

   a. Should the speech, dress, attitude or lifestyle of a Christian woman resemble the Immoral Woman's in any way?

      Yes   No

   b. Does God care what we wear?

      Yes   No

   c. Do you think it's possible to dress in a stylish, fashionable way and remain within God's dress code?

      Yes   No

Flirting, flattering, and flaunting it. That's how the Immoral Woman attracts guys. So, maybe you're wondering, "How can a biblically beautiful girl attract a guy?" Well, hang on until we get to Week 5, because in that lesson you're not only going to learn how to attract a guy, you're going to learn how to attract a great guy. So stay tuned to our study, and don't miss out on Week 5. But for now, I want you to get the inside scoop about what Christian guys think about modesty and the way girls dress and behave.

5. Alex and Brett Harris (a couple of young, Christian brothers) write a great blog that has blossomed into a movement called "The Rebelution," a "teenage rebellion against low expectations." In response to readers of their blog and discussions on their forums, a modesty survey was conducted to help girls understand how their dress affects guys. The girls submitted questions, the guys responded, and the survey results have been posted online. So here's your assignment:

- Go online right now to www.therebelution.com/modestysurvey/browse.

- In the "select a category" box, click several of the links to see the results of how what you wear and how you behave affects guys. Spend a few minutes browsing the survey results.

- Considering what you've just learned from the Modesty Survey, please answer the following questions:

a. According to the survey, how does the way a girl dresses affect a guy?

b. What are the three most practical things you learned from the survey that will help you dress more modestly?

c. According to the survey, modesty isn't just about what you wear. What are some of the other ways you can display modesty especially when you're around guys?

6. What insights has the Lord revealed to you today, and what does He want you to do with them?

reflect

NOTE: Another excellent online source that addresses the subject of modesty and Christian dress is an article entitled *Modesty Heart Check*. It includes some fantastic guidelines to help you make godly decisions about how to dress. You really need to check it out. You can find the link to this article at www.girltalk.blogs.com in the April 18, 2006 blog entry. Many of the April 2006 entries deal with the subject of modesty and fashion as well, and I highly recommend that you read and share them with others. The *GirlTalk* blog is one of my favorites.

Day Three

pray

1. As you can see by today's Proverb, the old "ignorance is bliss" philosophy is a lie. In fact, Jesus said, "You shall know the truth, and the truth shall make you free" (John 8:32 *NASB*). Spend a few moments in prayer thanking God for the wisdom, knowledge, and truth He's given you through His liberating, life-changing Word.

> *Wisdom will enter your heart,*
> *and knowledge will fill you with joy.*
> —Proverbs 2:10

Yesterday, you read a very descriptive passage about the Immoral Woman (Proverbs 7). When I studied that passage, I saw something that stunned me. It was in verse 14 where the Immoral Woman says, "I've offered my sacrifices and just finished my vows." I'd seen that verse before but, until then, I'd never noticed the dark reality it reveals: the Immoral Woman is a religious, churchgoing woman.

Don't get me wrong. I'm not saying the Immoral Woman in Proverbs 7 is a Christian. I don't believe she is. But here's what I do know: she does attend church, and she is religious. And based upon Proverbs 7:15 (where she says, "It's you I was looking for!"), I believe she goes to church to hunt for her next victim.

How does all of this apply to you? First of all, you need to be cautious in your relationships (even in your church relationships) because the Immoral Woman has the ability to deceive guys and girls alike. She may even want to be your best friend, so beware.

Secondly, examine your own heart and habits. Are you consciously or unconsciously imitating the Immoral Woman's behavior in your interactions and relationships with guys—even, perhaps, with guys in your church? Girl, don't even go there.

You've seen how the Immoral Woman dresses, speaks, and behaves, but how did she get this way? Where did it all begin? The answers to these questions are critical because they can prevent you from following in her footsteps. So let's get answers from the best and most reliable source of all time: Jesus.

2. Read Mark 7:21–23, and answer the following questions:

   a. According to Jesus, where does immorality (and every other sin) begin?

   b. Your answer to the previous question reveals how the Immoral Woman became an immoral woman. So, how can you keep from following in her footsteps?

In the passage you just read, Jesus used the term "sexual immorality" (your Bible may say "adulteries" or "fornications"). You need to know exactly what this means. As an unmarried teen, sexual immorality means any form of pre-marital sexual behavior. And if you get married someday, sexual immorality also means any form of sexual behavior with anyone other than your husband. Therefore, according to Jesus, sex in any form is prohibited unless you are married, and if you're married, sex may only be practiced with your spouse.

You've seen where immorality begins, now discover even more about what Jesus says about sex.

3. Read Matthew 5:27–28, and answer the following questions:

    a. How did Jesus broaden the definition of immorality/adultery in verse 28?

    b. In this passage, Jesus is speaking to guys, but would His message also apply to girls? Circle your answer.

    Yes   No

    c. So, when you see a good-looking guy (or when you're even thinking about a guy) what should you be careful NOT to do and why?

4. What about when a guy looks and lusts after a girl who dresses immodestly or flirts overtly? Is he the only one guilty of immorality? Once again, let's find answers to these questions from Jesus. Read Matthew 18:7, and answer those questions in the space below.

> *What sorrow awaits the world, because it tempts people to sin.*
> *Temptations are inevitable, but what sorrow awaits the person*
> *who does the tempting.* —Matthew 18:7

5. In today's culture, sexual temptation is everywhere. Temptation itself is not a sin, but giving in to the temptation (or being the actual tempter) is. Listed below are several very common ways we experience sexual temptation. Complete each sentence by describing a practical way you can resist the temptation and flee from sexual immorality.

    •   Immoral thoughts and fantasies: I can flee this temptation by _____
        _____

    •   Immoral television programs: I can flee this temptation by _____
        _____
        _____

    •   Immoral internet sites and ads: I can flee this temptation by _____
        _____

    •   Immoral reading material (magazines and books): I can flee this temptation by
        _____
        _____

    •   Immoral movies: I can flee this temptation by _____
        _____

    •   Guys who are flirtatious and/or sexually suggestive in their behavior: I can flee
        this temptation by _____
        _____

    •   Girls whose conversation or behavior is sexually suggestive or explicit: I can
        flee this temptation by _____
        _____

    I want to recommend a great resource to you. Covenant Eyes (www.covenanteyes.com) is an internet integrity and accountability program. It monitors every website your computer visits and sends periodic emailed reports of each site visited to an accountability partner of your choice. It's a great way to help you, your family members, or friends to "flee immorality." Check it out!

6. As a result of today's study, what has the Lord revealed to you about the importance of keeping your heart and mind pure?

_____

_____

_____

Day Four

1. God is so proud of you! You're taking time today to give Him and His Word priority, and it will make such a difference in your life. I trust you're already seeing the blessings of seeking Him first. Spend a few moments in prayer, thanking Him for enriching your life with His love, wisdom, and guidance.

> *(Wisdom) offers you life in her right hand,*
> *and riches and honor in her left.*
> *She will guide you down delightful paths;*
> *all her ways are satisfying.*
> —Proverbs 3:16–17

In today's world, immorality is the new normality. Retailers, advertisers, TV shows, and the music industry target you with messages that encourage, emphasize, and expect you to be sexually active. And despite the fact that sexually transmitted diseases and teen pregnancy rates are soaring, many people continue to preach the "safe sex" message.

But, precious girl, your heavenly Father wants so much more for you than the world does. As a Father, He wants to protect you and provide the best plan possible for your life. That's why He's given you His Word. He wants to tell you how to live in a way that will please Him and bless you and your future. Listen to Him today, and never forget: He loves you to pieces!

2. Why is sexual purity so important to God? Discover why by reading
    1 Corinthians 6:12–20.

1 Corinthians 6:12–20

12 *You say, "I am allowed to do anything"—but not everything is good for you. And
    even though "I am allowed to do anything," I must not become a slave to anything.*
13 *You say, "Food was made for the stomach, and the stomach for food." (This is true,
    though someday God will do away with both of them.) But you can't say that our
    bodies were made for sexual immorality. They were made for the Lord, and the
    Lord cares about our bodies.*
14 *And God will raise us from the dead by his power, just as he raised our Lord from
    the dead.*
15 *Don't you realize that your bodies are actually parts of Christ? Should a man take
    his body, which is part of Christ, and join it to a prostitute? Never!*
16 *And don't you realize that if a man joins himself to a prostitute, he becomes one
    body with her? For the Scriptures say, "The two are united into one."*
17 *But the person who is joined to the Lord is one spirit with him.*
18 *Run from sexual sin! No other sin so clearly affects the body as this one does.
    For sexual immorality is a sin against your own body.*
19 *Don't you realize that your body is the temple of the Holy Spirit, who lives in you
    and was given to you by God? You do not belong to yourself,*
20 *for God bought you with a high price. So you must honor God with your body.*

3. Using 1 Corinthians 6:12–20, answer the following questions:

    a. What did you learn about your body in verse 13?

    b. What did you learn about your body and sexual immorality from verses 15–18?

    c. What clear instruction is given regarding sexual immorality in verse 18?

d. Why is sexual immorality more serious and detrimental than other kinds of sin (verses 13–18)?

e. Who owns the rights to your body, and what is your responsibility regarding your body (verses 19–20)?

4. The standard for Christian sexuality is stated very simply in 1 Thessalonians 4:3-7. Please read this passage, and answer the questions that follow:

> *³ God's will is for you to be holy, so stay away from all sexual sin.*
> *⁴ Then each of you will control his own body and live in holiness and honor—*
> *⁵ not in lustful passion like the pagans who do not know God and his ways.*
> *⁶ Never harm or cheat a Christian brother in this matter by violating his wife, for the Lord avenges all such sins, as we have solemnly warned you before.*
> *⁷ God has called us to live holy lives, not impure lives.*
> —1 Thessalonians 4:3–7

a. What is God's will and sexual standard for you (verses 3a and 7)?

b. What does God instruct you to control and how (verses 3b-4)?

c. What are the consequences of sexual immorality (verse 6)?

5. I cannot close today's study without directing you to one more very important scripture. Pick up your Bible and turn to Hebrews 13:4. Please write that verse (and the warning it contains) in the space below.

6. Respond to everything your heavenly Father has taught you today by writing Him a brief note.

reflect
{

Dear Father, _____

_____

_____

_____

Day Five

pray
{

1. Reach out to God today through prayer, embracing Him and the wisdom He's given you this week.

*Wisdom is a tree of life
to those who embrace her;
happy are those who hold her tightly.*
—Proverbs 3:18

Is there hope for an Immoral Woman? Can God forgive an Immoral Woman? Yes and yes! God can and will forgive immorality. But what's more, He can still use us in spite of our past sin…and aren't you glad? Me, too!

If you're struggling with past sin and immorality, may today's study encourage your heart, renew your hope, and reignite your joy.

2. Matthew 1 records the genealogy of Jesus. Read Matthew 1:3–6, then record the female name(s) (mothers) mentioned in the blanks below.

Matthew 1:3–6

³ *Judah was the father of Perez and Zerah (whose mother was Tamar). Perez was the father of Hezron. Hezron was the father of Ram.*
⁴ *Ram was the father of Amminadab. Amminadab was the father of Nahshon. Nahshon was the father of Salmon.*
⁵ *Salmon was the father of Boaz (whose mother was Rahab). Boaz was the father of Obed (whose mother was Ruth). Obed was the father of Jesse.*
⁶ *Jesse was the father of King David. David was the father of Solomon (whose mother was Bathsheba, the widow of Uriah).*

Matthew 1:3 _____

Matthew 1:5 _____ and _____

Matthew 1:6 _____

Each of these women has something in common: immorality. One disguised herself and seduced her father-in-law (Genesis 38:13–18). Another was a prostitute (Joshua 2:1). One was raised in a city where her family participated in an idolatrous, immoral form of religion (Ruth 1:15). The other committed adultery (2 Samuel 11:2–5).

But immorality isn't the only thing these women have in common. They also shared a common faith in God that led them to repent of their sin and receive His forgiveness. Then God went even one step further. He gave each of them a place in the genealogy of His only begotten Son, Jesus. Why did He do that? I believe He did it to show you and me the "surpassing riches of His grace in kindness toward us in Christ Jesus" (Ephesians 2:7 *NASB*).

All of us need to receive God's forgiveness and grace for our sin, but how can we? The only way possible is by accepting God's gift of salvation through faith in Christ (Ephesians 2:8). You see, Jesus died for our sins, was buried, and rose from the dead to give us salvation, forgiveness from our sins, and eternal life.

Have you ever received God's forgiveness and salvation? God wants you to. Romans 10:9–10 says, "If you confess with your mouth that Jesus is Lord and believe in your heart that God raised him from the dead you will be saved. For it is by believing in your heart that you are made right with God, and it is by confessing with your mouth that you are saved."

If you'd like to receive God's gift of salvation, you can. Right now, tell Him that you want to be forgiven for your sins. Tell Him that you believe Jesus died to save you and rose from the dead to give you eternal life. Invite Him to come into your heart and save you. And when you do that, He will not only save and forgive you, He will also send His Spirit to live within you to enable you to live a life that glorifies and pleases Him (1 Corinthians 6:19–20).

Perhaps you've been a Christian for a while, and maybe you're wondering if God can forgive you of the sins you've committed since you became a Christian. Maybe even the sin of immorality. Absolutely! Truth is, when you were saved God forgave you for ALL of your sins past, present, and future. And here's some awesome news: Your sin cannot affect your salvation or your eternal relationship with God (John 10:28–29).

However, when you sin as a Christian, you grieve and quench the Spirit of God. He responds by convicting you of your sin in order to encourage you to repent and restore fellowship (not relationship – that was settled at salvation) with God. And here's more good news: The Bible says, "If we confess our sins to him, he is faithful and just to forgive us our sins and to cleanse us from all wickedness" (1 John 1:9). If He's convicting you of sin you've never confessed, I encourage you to respond to Him right now. Confess your sin to God and turn away from it. He will forgive and cleanse you, and you will enjoy restored fellowship with Him and a fresh infilling of His Spirit.

3. You've seen the names of several immoral women in the genealogy of Jesus, but pick up your Bible and take a look at Romans 8:15–17. Record what you learn about your own spiritual genealogy. It's beautiful!

4. I want you to look at one final passage today. Read John 8:3–11, and answer the following questions:

    a. How is the woman in this passage described (verse 3)?

    b. What was Jesus' response and instruction to the woman (verses 10–11)?

    c. What is Jesus teaching us in this passage regarding immorality and any other sin?

5. As you conclude this second week of study, take a few minutes to journal what the Lord has done in your heart by completing the following sentence:

reflect

⎰ *This week the Lord...* _____

_____

_____

_____

_____

_____

_____

_____

I learned how to study the Bible from a former Immoral Woman. Kay Arthur—Bible teacher, author, and cofounder of Precept Ministries—is that woman. And I am only one of the thousands upon thousands of lives God has enabled Kay to reach and teach.

Many years ago, when she was a young wife and mother, Kay's husband committed suicide. Soon after that, she spiraled into an immoral lifestyle. She was desperately searching for love, but all she found was sorrow—until she met Jesus. After that, everything about her changed. She hungered for God and began devouring His Word. She became a godly woman—a biblically beautiful woman—and eventually, God led Kay to her husband, Jack Arthur.

Several years after they married, Kay and Jack founded Precept Ministries, and God has blessed, multiplied and grown it into a worldwide outreach. All over the globe, people have learned how to study God's Word through the Bible studies Kay has written and through the excellent training Precept provides.

My dear sister, don't let your past define your present or prevent you from God's plan for your future. Accept His grace and forgiveness through the blood of His Son. Become the biblically beautiful woman He wants you to be. I am so grateful Kay Arthur did.

Week Two • *The Immoral Woman vs. The Godly Woman*

Biblical Beauty Don't: The Immoral Woman:

1) *How does she speak?* Prov. 2:16, 5:3, 7:5, 15, 21

   _____, flirtatious, flattering, and enticing.

2) *How does she act?* Prov. 7:10–16

   _____, brash, rebellious.

3) *How does she dress?* Prov. 7:10

   Seductively, _____, inappropriately.

4) *What is her heart like?* Prov. 5:6, 30:20, 7:14

   Religious but _____ God's ways;

   she _____ and destroys others with no remorse.

5) *What is her destiny?* Prov. 5:5, 7:27

   Destruction, death, and _____.

Biblical Beauty Do: The Godly Woman:

1) *How does she speak?* 1 Peter 3:4

   _____, _____, discreet, and edifying.

2) *How does she act?* 1 Peter 3:2, 1 Thess. 4:3–7

   Avoids sexual _____, controls her body so as not to

   _____ others.

   Defraud = *to take advantage of someone; to cause someone to stumble.*

3) *How does she dress?* 1 Timothy 2:9–10

   _____, decently, and _____.

4) *What is her heart like?* 1 Thess. 4:1, 7

   Longs to _____ God and lead a holy life.

5) *What is her destiny?* 1 Thess. 5:9–10

   Eternal life, salvation, and the _____ of God's blessing.

Week 3 · *The Indiscreet Woman*

"Granmuhver." It's my new favorite word. It took Ezra, my grandson, almost two years to be able to say it. "Nana" or "Mimi" would have been much easier for him to master, but I come from a long line of "Grandmothers," so that particular title was dear to me. For months and months, Ezra struggled with the formidable three-syllable word. But his perseverance paid off this week as "Granmuhver" rolled off his tongue to the cheers of the very one he addressed.

I think one of the reasons God gives us grandchildren is to give us a second chance to learn what we somehow failed to learn with our own children. Watching Ezra struggle to learn my name has given me a new understanding of God's patience with me.

When I was a young woman, I spent way too much time beating myself up for my failures and lack of spiritual progress. And at times I thought God was even more put out with me than I was. But as a grandmother, I now see what God likely saw back then. He saw me striving and persevering to grow and mature as a Christian, but He also saw there were many formidable three-syllable disciplines that I couldn't master yet…so He patiently waited as I grew.

God's patience. Our perseverance. These are the principles I want to plant in your heart as we begin this week's lesson on the topic of "discretion"—another formidable three-syllable word. It cannot be attained overnight, but as we persevere and God patiently watches, we can become biblically beautiful women of discretion. Little sister, let's persevere 'til we hear God's cheer.

> *Well done, my good and faithful servant.*
> —Matthew 25:21

Day One

1. As you can see by today's Proverb, Wisdom's friends are Prudence, Knowledge, and Discretion. Pray, asking God to show you how to make them your friends, too.

   > *"I, wisdom, dwell together with prudence;*
   > *I possess knowledge and discretion."*
   > —Proverbs 8:12 *NIV*

Allow me to re-introduce you to our Beauty Don't #2, the **Indiscreet Woman**. Unlike the Immoral Woman who is given so much space in the Proverbs, the Indiscreet Woman is only mentioned once. But that single verse packs a real punch. You read it in Week One, but just in case you've forgotten, here it is:

> *A woman who is beautiful but lacks discretion*
> *is like a gold ring in a pig's snout.*
> —Proverbs 11:22

It's kind of funny at first (can't you just picture a proud pig wearing a pretty gold ring?), but that passage isn't just intended to amuse. This proverbial put down also contains a powerful message about the necessity of discretion.

There may only be one verse dedicated to the Indiscreet Woman, but there are plenty of verses in Proverbs that instruct and exhort us to obtain discretion and prudence. Today you'll discover why you need both.

2. Turn back to Week 1, Day 2, number 2, and reacquaint yourself with the definition of "discretion" by reviewing its synonyms.

   In Proverbs 11:22, the word "discretion" means "taste, judgment, and discernment."[3] It can also mean "mental or spiritual perception or discernment."[4] This means the beautiful woman in Proverbs 11:22 had poor taste, bad judgment, no discernment, and lacked mental or spiritual perception. Add all of those ingredients together and you've got a recipe for a disastrous life! Can you see why discretion is so important?

3. Read Proverbs 3:21–26, and record what you learn about the benefits of discretion and the specific ways it can protect you.

   NOTE: Depending on your Bible translation, the word "discretion" may be translated as wise/wisdom, prudent, discernment, or sensible.

4. What does discretion look like? How does a young woman of discretion behave? And most importantly, how can you know whether or not you possess discretion? The answers to these questions are found in Proverbs as Solomon contrasts the behavior of the discreet and prudent with the foolish, simple, and naïve.

   Read the following verses from Proverbs noting what you learn about the behavior of the discreet versus the behavior of the fool. Keep in mind that prudence, wisdom, and knowledge are synonyms of discretion. To give you a head start, I've completed the first one for you.

   NOTE: To enhance your understanding, you may want to read each verse from two or three Bible translations. One of the simplest ways to access a variety of translations is by visiting www.biblegateway.com. It will also make completing the chart much easier.

Read:	A discreet/prudent person...	But a fool/simple person...
Prov. 12:16	*overlooks or remains calm when insulted*	*gets angry fast*
Prov. 13:16		
Prov. 14:15		
Prov. 15:5		
Prov. 22:3		

5. Ask God to show you one or two specific areas in your life where you need to develop discretion and prudence. Record your insights.

reflect {

_____

_____

_____

_____

Day Two

discretion
prudence
wisdom

pray {

1. You have influence. Whether it's with your friends or family, your life influences others. Are you advising them wisely? Are you helping them succeed? Your responsibility as a young woman of influence is huge. Get on your knees right now and ask God to give you wisdom in your relationships, conversations and dealings with others.

> *"Good advice and success belong to me (wisdom).*
> *Insight and strength are mine.*
> *Because of me, kings reign, and rulers make just laws.*
> *Rulers lead with my help, and nobles make righteous judgments."*
> —Proverbs 8:14–16

We spent yesterday entirely in Proverbs, but today we are going to get out and meet one of the most fascinating women in the Bible. Her name is Abigail, and she's a role model of discretion, prudence and wisdom. I think you're going to love her. She's certainly taught me a lot—can't wait to meet her one day! Enjoy your time today with Abigail.

2. Pick up your Bible and get to know Abigail by reading 1 Samuel 25:1–42, then record your insights to the following questions:

a. What kind of woman was Abigail? How was she described (verse 3)?

b.   What was her husband like (verse 3)?

c.   When David's men requested payment for services they had provided to Nabal (they had protected Nabal's shepherds and his sheep), Nabal foolishly refused to pay (verses 4–11). As a result, David and his men planned to kill Nabal and his entire household (verses 12–13, 21–22). But one of Nabal's servants told Abigail about everything that was about to happen and asked her to get involved. What did Abigail do (verses 18–31)?

d.   How did Abigail's actions and speech reveal her discretion, prudence, and wisdom?

e.   What immediate benefits did Abigail receive because of her discretion and prudence (verses 34–35)?

f. What happened to Nabal (verses 37–38)?

g. What future benefits did Abilgail receive because of her discretion and prudence (verses 39–42)?

3. We all have to deal with foolish, difficult people at times. What insights did you learn from Abigail to help you deal with the Nabals in your life?

reflect {

_____

_____

_____

_____

Day Three

1. As you read today's Proverb, I hope you are encouraged by God's invitation to freely give you wisdom. Take Him up on His offer. Ask Him to give you wisdom as you study His Word today.

    Listen as Wisdom calls out! Hear as understanding raises her voice!
    … At the entrance to the city, at the city gates, she cries aloud,
    "I call to you, to all of you! I am raising my voice to all people.
    How naïve you are! Let me give you some common sense.
    O foolish ones, let me give you understanding."
    —Proverbs 8:1–5

"Discretion" used to be one of those innocuous, vanilla-sounding words that I associated with…well, "boring." I knew it was closely related to the word "prudent" (another unpopular, seldom-used word) but to be honest, both words were a little yawn inducing to me. Not anymore.

God's Word has completely changed the negative connotations I used to associate with the words "discretion" and "prudence." Although I don't often use those specific words (and I'm guessing you probably don't either), I do use positive terms like "smart," "discerning," "spiritually sharp," and "wise" to describe discreet, prudent people.

Whatever you may choose to call them, discretion and prudence are keys that can unlock your God-given potential. My goal today is to take you into God's Word where He can whet your appetite to live up to that potential. My prayer is that you will take what He teaches you and run with it.

2. Yesterday, when you studied Abigail, you also met David. Today, we'll go back to an earlier period of David's life when he was a young shepherd living at home with his family. Read 1 Samuel 16:14–22 and answer the following questions:

   a. In this passage, you learned that David was a skillful musician, but what did you learn about his character (verse 18)?

   b. What was the result of David's discretion and prudence (verses 19–22)?

3. Joseph, another Old Testament character, was a young man whose jealous brothers sold him to slave traders who, in turn, took him to Egypt. While he was there, Joseph was wrongly convicted and jailed. But because of his God-given ability to interpret dreams, he was eventually summoned to appear before Pharaoh to interpret Pharaoh's dream. Read Genesis 41:38–44, and answer the following questions:

    a.   What did you learn about Joseph's character in this passage (verses 38–39)?

    b.   What was the result of Joseph's discretion, discernment, and wisdom (verses 40–44)?

4.   David and Joseph were both young when they began serving King Saul and Pharaoh. What does this reveal about discretion, wisdom, and discernment? Before you answer this question, read Proverbs 20:11 for additional insight (and keep in mind, this verse applies to both guys and gals).

5.   As a young woman, what insights have you learned today to apply to your own life? How are you doing when it comes to discretion?

reflect

Day Four

1. One of the things I love the most about the incredibly prudent group of Old Testament characters we have studied over the past two days is their humility. Humble yourself before the Lord today in prayer, and ask Him to help you stay that way.

   Don't be impressed with your own wisdom.
   Instead, fear the Lord and turn away from evil.
   —Proverbs 3:7

In your study of Abigail, David, and Joseph, you have seen real-life examples of what discretion looks like. You have also seen the powerful way God can use those who possess it. Today you will meet another incredible Old Testament character: Daniel.

It is my heartfelt prayer that God will use Abigail, David, Joseph, and Daniel to inspire and encourage you to become a modern-day example of discretion before your family and friends. May all who know you witness the biblical beauty mark of discretion upon your life.

2. Daniel was a young Jewish teen who was taken into Babylonian captivity where he served King Nebuchadnezzar. One night, the king had a dream, and none of his magicians or wise men could interpret it. As a result, Nebuchadnezzar ordered their deaths and the deaths of Daniel and his friends. Read the following passages and questions, and record what you learn:

   a. Daniel 2:12–19—What did you learn about Daniel's character (verses 14, 16–19)?

   b. Daniel 2:46–48—What was the result of Daniel's wisdom, discretion, and prudence?

3. Joseph, David, Abigail, and Daniel all shared: 1) a common faith in God, and 2) the attributes of discretion, prudence, discernment, and wisdom. But there's something else they shared in common, and here's a hint: what happened to each of them after their discretion and prudence was recognized by others?

Friendships are so important but, sadly, a lack of discretion can destroy even the best of friendships. Girl, let's just call it what it really is: gabbing and gossiping. We've both been guilty of it, and we've both been hurt by it. Our final study today will remind us of the dangers of indiscretion and the blessings of just plain ol' keeping our mouths shut.

4. Read the following scriptures, and record what you learn about the dangers of indiscretion, the blessings of discretion, and how to preserve precious friendships:

   a. Proverbs 11:13

   b. Proverbs 16:28

   c. Proverbs 17:9

d. Proverbs 21:23

e. Proverbs 26:20

5. Have you ever been hurt by gossip? If so, describe the damage it did and the toll it took on you. Also, describe how it affected your relationship with the gossip.

6. Finally, as you reflect upon your own relationships, how and with whom are you most challenged to be discreet? What specific, scriptural steps can you take to become a woman of discretion and not a gossip?

reflect

_____

_____

_____

_____

Day Five

pray

1. Everyone wants to have joy, and those who follow wisdom usually do. Take a few minutes to praise and thank God for the joy He has brought you, and for the sorrow He has saved you from all because of the wisdom He has given you.

> *"My children, listen to me (wisdom),*
> *for all who follow my ways are joyful.*
> *…Joyful are those who listen to me,*
> *watching for me daily at my gates,*
> *waiting for me outside my home."*
> —Proverbs 8:32–34

Discretion and prudence are in short supply in today's world. Are you ready to begin making up for that deficit? You can. God has given you everything you need to become a woman of influence and discretion. And as you have seen in your homework this week, one discreet woman can make a huge difference in so many lives. May your study today encourage you to step up and be that woman.

2. Prudence and discretion are synonymous with wisdom, and one of the most encouraging promises about wisdom is found in James 1:5–8. Find out how to get wisdom by reading this passage and answering the following questions:

> [5] *If you need wisdom, ask our generous God,*
> *and He will give it to you. He will not*
> *rebuke you for asking..*
> [6] *But when you ask Him, be sure that your faith is in God alone.*
> *Do not waver, for a person with divided loyalty is as unsettled as a*
> *wave of the sea that is blown and tossed by the wind.*
> [7] *Such people should not expect to receive anything from the Lord.*
> [8] *Their loyalty is divided between God and the world, and they are unstable*
> *in everything they do.*

a. How can you receive wisdom (verse 5)?

b. Who is the source of wisdom (verse 5)?

c. What are the requirements for receiving wisdom (verse 6a)?

d. Who should not expect to receive wisdom (verses 6b–8)?

e. So, what's the first thing you should do the next time you need wisdom?

3. Now let's focus on two other areas in your life that will greatly determine your ability to grow in wisdom and discretion. Read the following verses and record what you learn about how to grow in wisdom:

a. Psalm 119:97–100

b.   Proverbs 13:20

c.   1 Peter 2:2

    Girl, you're on your way to becoming a biblical beauty because guess what? You've just completed the first half of our study. Thank you for your dedication and commitment! I'm so proud of you!

    My favorite Old Testament verse says, "And He humbled you and let you be hungry, and fed you with manna which you did not know, nor did your fathers know, that He might make you understand that man does not live by bread alone, but man lives by everything that proceeds out of the mouth of the Lord" (Deuteronomy 8:3 *NASB*). I'm praying you're feeling really full right now because of the feast God has fed you over the past three weeks. God bless you for giving His Word priority!

4.   Spend a few minutes journaling what the Lord has done in your heart this week through His Word by completing the following sentence:

reflect {

This week the Lord... _____

_____

_____

_____

_____

_____

_____

I was having a very difficult time with a very difficult person. Nothing I could say or do seemed to improve the relationship, and I could not understand why. It was a puzzle I could not solve. What I needed was a great, big, heaping dose of discretion—but I didn't know that. Thank God, He did. And He knew just the woman who could give it to me.

One evening while I was at a friend's house, I picked up a book she had by an author I had heard of but had never read before. As I perused through its pages, I was astonished; it described my difficult relationship in detail. I borrowed that book, took it straight home, and read it all night. And somewhere in the wee hours of the morning, God used the words of that author to give me the wisdom I needed to deal with that relationship the right way. The prudent way. The discreet way.

Since that time, I have read almost every book Jan Silvious has written. A gifted author, speaker, and Christian counselor, Jan is also an amazing woman of discretion and discernment. I am serious when I tell you that you need to get your hands on every book she has written. Practical, biblical, witty, and intelligent, Jan epitomizes the biblically beautiful attributes of prudence and discretion.

As I've said before, we can't become women of discretion overnight. But spending time with wonderful authors like Jan Silvious can get us there a whole lot faster.

Want to find out more about

Jan Silvious
and her books?

Visit her online at
www.jansilvious.com

Week Three • *The Indiscreet Woman vs. The Woman of Discretion*

OT synonyms for discretion:
discreet, discerning, prudent, understanding, insight, wise

NT synonyms for discretion:
discreet, sensible, sober, self-controlled, wisdom

Biblical Beauty Don't:
The Indiscreet Woman:

1) She _____ too much and _____ whatever comes into her head.

2) She _____ at personal and _____ growth.

3) She makes _____ _____ based on bad judgment.

4) She's _____ and enjoys _____.

5) She _____ with danger and _____ it.

Biblical Beauty Do:
The Discreet Woman:

1) She _____ her _____ and speaks with wisdom. *Prov. 10:13, 11:12*

2) She's eager to learn, _____, and mature _____. *Prov. 14:6*

3) She makes _____ _____ based on truth. *Prov. 13:16, 14:15*

4) She is _____-_____ and not easily angered. *Prov. 17:27*

5) She _____ danger and _____ it. *Prov. 27:12*

Week 4 • *The Irritating Woman*

Wouldn't you know it. Mere seconds before I began writing this lesson on the Beauty Don't #3—the **Irritating Woman**—I opened my mouth and became that woman. I should have seen it coming.

Clue #1: My husband Bill had been doing a small home repair project. Home repair projects seldom go smoothly at the Cole house. This should have alerted me to the very real possibility that things could be heading south fast.

Clue #2 came in the form of a question: "Do we have an X-ACTO® knife?" Bill asked. Scary. So, I took a deep breath and replied, "Yes, it's in the pantry in the tool drawer." But I knew I should also have said, "Let me go get it and bring it to you." But I didn't. I didn't want to. "Let him get it," I thought to myself. "He's a big boy." And that sassy little selfish attitude was Clue #3—I should have known what was about to happen.

Less than five minutes later, that contentious, crabby Irritating Woman appeared.

I walked into the room where Bill was doing the repair, and to my absolute horror I discovered he wasn't using an X-ACTO® knife. No, turns out, he couldn't find the X-ACTO® knife so he was using one of my very best kitchen knives. That man was carving into drywall with my good knife! Gasping then erupting, I exploded. Words gushed from my mouth…followed by silence. Too much silence if you know what I mean.

Fortunately, I have a very forgiving husband. After I apologized, peace prevailed. But oh, how I hate it when I foolishly ignore every obvious clue around me and give in to the Irritating Woman.

I wonder. Has the Irritating Woman shown up at your house lately? Have your friends or teachers ever met her? Wouldn't you like to banish bossy ol' Beauty Don't #3 and replace her with her biblically beautiful counterpart the Edifying Woman? Well then, this lesson is for you. Oh, who am I kidding? This lesson is for me, too.

Day One

pray

1. The message of today's proverb is obvious. Ask God to take the limp out of your spiritual walk by committing to be led by His wisdom.

> *If you live a life guided by wisdom,*
> *you won't limp or stumble as you run.*
> —Proverbs 4:12

The Irritating Woman is mentioned five times in Proverbs, and each time it says practically the same thing. So why would God repeat Himself five times?

I believe it's because He wants to emphasize a message that He doesn't want us girls to miss.

But I think there's another reason why God mentions the Irritating Woman five times. It's because He loves us—and He "gets" us girls, too. Hold on to that thought as we begin our study of the ugly, unlikable woman none of us want to be, Beauty Don't #3.

2. Read each verse about the Irritating Woman, and answer the questions that follow.

   NOTE: The verses below are taken from the *New Living Translation*, but in other Bible translations, the word "woman" is used instead of "wife." Therefore, these verses apply to all women of all ages, not just married women. Also, the word "contentious" means quarrelsome and argumentative.[5]

   A nagging wife annoys like a constant dripping.
   —Proverbs 19:13

   *It is better to live alone in the corner of an attic
   than with a contentious wife in a lovely home.*
   —Proverbs 21:9

   *It is better to live alone in the desert
   than with a crabby, complaining wife.*
   —Proverbs 21:19

   *It is better to live alone in the corner of an attic
   than with a quarrelsome wife in a lovely home.*
   —Proverbs 25:24

   *A quarrelsome wife is as annoying as
   a constant dripping on a rainy day.
   Stopping her complaints is like trying to stop the wind
   or trying to hold something with greased hands.*
   —Proverbs 27:15–16

   a. How is the Irritating Woman described? Answer this question by circling the specific adjectives used to describe her in the verses above.

   b. Now let's broaden our perspective about the Irritating Woman. What are some synonyms for the words you just circled? What do you call a girl or woman like this (careful!)? Record several synonyms.

c. As you look at the words you circled and the synonyms you found, it's easy to see the downside of having to hang out with an Irritating Woman whether she's young or old. In fact, three of the five verses begin with the same six words, and they describe exactly how she makes other people feel. Record those words in the blanks below.

_____ _____ _____ _____ _____ _____

d. Think about the six words you just recorded, and answer these questions: If that's how an irritating girl or woman makes people feel, what choice will they eventually make? What will ultimately happen to her?

3. One example of the dangerous consequences of becoming an Irritating Woman is found in 2 Samuel 6:12-23. It details an encounter between King David and his wife, Michal. Read this passage, picturing it in your mind as you read, and answer the following questions:

    NOTE: An ephod (v. 14) was a simple robe worn primarily by priests of that day. Therefore, David was not uncovered as Michal sarcastically claimed (v. 20).

    a. What did David do that provoked Michal, and what does this reveal about her heart and her own relationship with the Lord (verse 16a)?

    b. Before Michal ever said a word to David, what had she already done (verse 16b)?

c. Note how the conversation between Michal and David began (verse 20). Who started it, and what does this tell you?

d. How would you describe Michal's words to David?

e. What consequences did Michal experience in her life and marriage as a result of her words and attitude (v. 23)?

I am embarrassed to share this, but I must confess. When I was your age, I spent way too much time in critical, complaining, Irritating Woman mode. I cut down and criticized others regularly, and I complained and whined about, well, almost everything.

When I think about the negativity and tension I caused in my relationships at home and at school back then, it makes me cringe. And you know what? That Irritating Woman never did really work for me. In fact, I'm pretty sure she worked against me. As I recall, my name never came anywhere close to making the ballot for Class Favorite. But if Class Critic had been up for vote, yikes!

4. So, what about you, my precious, young friend. Has the Irritating Woman shown up in your life lately? What will you do today to prevent from becoming a full-fledge, Irritating Woman deluxe (like Michal) in the future?

reflect

Day Two

1. The Irritating Woman seems to bring out the worst in others. Her crabbiness and contentiousness pushes everybody's buttons. So what can you do to prevent from being sucked in? To answer that question, read today's proverb. Then pray and ask God to protect you the next time an Irritating Woman starts to get on your last nerve.

Wisdom will save you from evil people,
from those whose speech is corrupt.
—Proverbs 2:12

Yesterday, you saw the dangers and consequences of becoming an Irritating Woman. She annoys and aggravates others, she offends her friends, and she can even undermine and destroy her own marriage. Anyone can see the fallout of her flawed behavior—a path of destruction follows her everywhere she goes. And if she refuses to change, her life will devolve into a series of broken relationships.

If the downside of becoming an Irritating Woman is so obvious, then why do we girls struggle so hard with giving in and becoming just like her? Let's get to the root of our universal problem in today's study.

2. Where did the Irritating Woman come from? Uncovering and understanding her past (and ours) will empower us from being overpowered by her. Genesis 3 records the fall of man—the sin of Adam and Eve—and the resulting consequences. Read God's words to Eve from the translations provided, and answer the questions that follow:

To the woman He said, "I will greatly multiply Your pain in childbirth,
In pain you will bring forth children; Yet your desire will be for your husband,
And he will rule over you."
—Genesis 3:16 (*NASB*)

Then he said to the woman, "I will sharpen the pain of your pregnancy,
and in pain you will give birth. And you will desire to control your husband,
but he will rule over you."
—Genesis 3:16

a. How did the fall (sin) change the dynamics of Eve's relationship with Adam?

b. Who has God called to be the leader of the home, and why is that such a challenge for women?

Genesis reveals the root problem of the Irritating Woman: sin and a desire to control others. It also opens the door to another topic that is a sore subject with some women: submission. Now I realize that marriage may be a long way off for you, but you're probably already thinking about Mr. Right and hoping to marry someday. But, precious girl, before you ever even meet him, you really need to know what the Bible teaches about submission. Why? Because it will help you choose the right Mr. Right!

The Bible teaches clearly that wives are to submit to their own husbands (not to every man, but to their own husbands). It also teaches that husbands are to love their wives as Christ loved the church (Ephesians 5:22–33). **Submission basically means that women are to respectfully place themselves under the authority of their husbands.** That's why it's so important that you choose the right kind of man to marry (which will be the focus of next week's lesson), a man whose authority you respect.

The scriptural principles of submission, however, *do not imply that women are inferior to men.* On the contrary, Scripture emphasizes the equality of men and women: "God created man in His own image, in the image of God He created Him; male and female He created them" (Genesis 1:27 *NASB*). But even before the fall of man, Adam and Eve had different roles. From the beginning, God created man to lead the home and woman to be his helper (Genesis 2:18). Eve's submission to Adam wasn't a problem before they sinned, but it became a major problem after they sinned.

Now just in case you're upset (or a little offended) by the concept of submission, please take time to read Philippians 2:5–11. This beautiful passage reveals that Christ—who is equal with God—willingly submitted Himself to God when He came to this earth and died on the cross to save us. In this way, Christ is an example to everyone (men and women alike) of the beauty and importance of submission.

One final point on this topic: submission is not unconditional. A wife is not required to submit to abuse or to ongoing sexual infidelity and immorality. When abuse occurs, a wife should seek protection from civil authorities as well as support from her church. When there is infidelity or immorality, a wife should seek sound, biblical Christian counsel.

Are married women the only ones who struggle with the desire to control others and the contentious, complaining attitude that desire breeds? No. Every woman young or old, single or married—every descendant of Eve—struggles with it, even spiritually mature women, and you're about to meet one of them.

3. Miriam was the older sister of Moses and Aaron. All three siblings were leaders over the Israelites, but God gave Moses authority over Miriam and Aaron (even though Moses was the youngest). God also chose Moses to be His #1 spokesman. A chilling encounter between Miriam, Aaron, and Moses is recorded in Numbers 12:1–15. Use your Bible to read this passage, and then answer the following questions:

   NOTE: Cushites were not Israelites, but Israelites were not prohibited by God from marrying Cushites.

a. What caused Miriam to become an Irritating Woman (v. 1-2)? In other words, what set her off?

b. What do Miriam's words reveal about her heart? Do you think jealousy could have been the root of her contentious, complaining behavior?

c. What do you think Miriam sought to gain by her quarrelsome complaints? In other words, what payoff do you think she was seeking?

d. What was Miriam's actual payoff (vs. 4–15)?

4. You've seen what set Miriam off, but think about yourself for a minute. Record one or two things that have set off the Irritating Woman in you lately.

5. Who are the primary earthly authority figures in your life (for example: your parents, teachers, church leaders, etc.). Write their names in the following blanks, and circle the phrase that best describes your current level of respect and attitude toward them.

	very respectful	mostly respectful	respect varies frequently	mostly disrespectful	very disrespectful
_____	very respectful	mostly respectful	respect varies frequently	mostly disrespectful	very disrespectful
_____	very respectful	mostly respectful	respect varies frequently	mostly disrespectful	very disrespectful
_____	very respectful	mostly respectful	respect varies frequently	mostly disrespectful	very disrespectful
_____	very respectful	mostly respectful	respect varies frequently	mostly disrespectful	very disrespectful
_____	very respectful	mostly respectful	respect varies frequently	mostly disrespectful	very disrespectful
_____	very respectful	mostly respectful	respect varies frequently	mostly disrespectful	very disrespectful

6. It's time to dethrone that cranky, critical, complaining Irritating Woman who wants to run (and possibly ruin) your life. If you've been an Irritating Woman lately, write a brief sentence confessing your sin to the Lord, and receive His forgiveness. Then take the next step: Ask anyone who has witnessed and/or been the object of your Irritating Woman behavior to forgive you.

reflect

_____

_____

_____

_____

Day Three

pray {

1. Wisdom wants to be your sister and best friend—and you could have none better. Ask God to help you get to know Wisdom well so that your friendship with her will flourish and bear much fruit.

> *Say to wisdom, "You are my sister,"*
> *and call insight your intimate friend.*
> —Proverbs 7:4 *RSV*

I don't know about you, but I'm worn out from spending the past two days with irritating women. First there was Michal who taught us how to lose a good man. Then there was Miriam who taught us how to rile God's anger through jealousy, envy, and a critical, complaining spirit.

So today, let's hang out with some cool-headed chicks you've probably never met before: Mahlah, Noah, Hoglah, Milcah and Tirzah, also known as "the daughters of Zelophehad." These gals really know how to handle themselves, and the beautiful thing about them is this: they know how to get what they want without crabbing, complaining, or controlling. By the time you've finished reading about them, you may even want to name one of your future daughters after them—probably not "Hoglah" though!

Enjoy your time with the five biblically beautiful daughters of Zelophehad.

2. Your assignment is simple. Read the following passages, and record your answers to the questions on the chart.

- Numbers 27:1–11: This passage tells about a meeting the sisters had with Moses. Their meeting occurred after a census had been taken to determine the adult male population of each tribe of Israel. Results from the census would enable Moses to determine how much land each tribe would receive. At that time, only males could inherit land.

- Numbers 36:1–12: This passage tells about another meeting Moses had with the male relatives of the daughters of Zelophehad.

The Daughters of Zelophehad

What problems and complications did they face (Num. 27:3–4, 36:1–4)?	How did they handle their problems, and what characteristics did they display?
How would an Irritating Woman handle problems like these?	How would others ultimately benefit from the way they handled their problem (Num. 27:8–11)?

3. What did you think about the daughters of Zelophehad, and what did the Holy Spirit teach you through their example about the right way to handle problems—especially problems dealing with injustice.

reflect

_____

_____

_____

_____

Day Four

pray

1. Today you'll be studying the power of the spoken word. Before you begin, pray and commit to speak life-giving, refreshing words to every person whose life will intersect yours today.

    A person's words can be life giving water;
    words of true wisdom are as refreshing as a bubbling brook.
    —Proverbs 18:4

Back in Week One, you learned about 3C Syndrome, a malady marked by Contentiousness, Crabbiness, and frequent bouts of Complaining—all of the primary symptoms of the Irritating Woman. 3C is easily identified and, as we've learned, all women struggle with it. But men are not immune from it either. Remember Aaron, Moses' brother? He had a pretty bad case of 3C himself.

This week you've discovered:

*   The dangers of 3C: destroyed relationships and God's judgment.

*   The source of 3C: the sin of your ancestors, Adam and Eve.

*   The root causes of 3C: the desire to control others, as well as jealousy, ambition, envy, etc.

Our goal today is to discover the cure for 3C. Yes, hallelujah, there is a cure! It's easily administered, available to everyone, and it can completely reverse the adverse effects of 3C. What is this miraculous remedy? It's something I call 3B. Curious about this cure-all? C'mon, let's get in the Word and get more info.

2. Read Ephesians 4:29.

> *Let no unwholesome word proceed from your mouth,*
> *but only such a word as is good for edification,*
> *according to the need of the moment, that it may give*
> *grace to those who hear.*
>
> —Ephesians 4:29 *NASB*

3. According to Ephesians 4:29, what are the only kind of words you are allowed to speak? Circle the answer in the verse.

Ephesians 4:29 gives us three divine boundaries for every word we speak. First, we must choose words that are "good" (*agathos* in the Greek), which is defined as "benevolent and beneficial."[6] Second, our words must "edify" (*oikodome* in the Greek), which means to "build up and spiritually profit" others.[7] The final criteria for the words we choose is that they must "give grace" (*charis* in the Greek), which means to bless and benefit others.[8]

In Dr. Spiros Zodhiates's wonderful resource, *The Complete Word Study Dictionary New Testament*, he defines grace like this:

Grace

A favor done without expectation of return; the absolutely free expression of the loving kindness of God to men finding its only motive in the bounty and benevolence of the Giver; unearned and unmerited favor.[9]

What does all of this mean to us? Very simply, it means that the words that flow from our lips must do three things: **build**, **bless**, and **benefit**. This is 3B speech—the cure for 3C. Furthermore, we're to speak these words in a way that illustrates and emulates God's grace, which means even if the hearer has not earned and does not deserve to hear 3B words, we must speak them anyway.

Do these boundaries mean that we cannot confront or correct others or honestly express ourselves to them? Absolutely not, but it does mean that we must do it in a positive, gracious way with the motivation of building up, not tearing down.

4. What do 3B words look and sound like? To discover practical examples of the specific kinds of words that build, bless, and benefit, let's return to Proverbs for a little lesson on "How to Speak 3B." Read each verse and complete the sentences. To help you get started, I've completed the first one for you.

How to Speak 3B	
Proverbs 10:11	*3B words...* give life to others
Proverbs 10:21, 12:25	*3B words...*
Proverbs 10:31–32	*3B words...*
Proverbs 15:1	*3B words...*
Proverbs 16:23	*3B words...*

5. Make a list below of the primary people your life touches on a daily basis, then take each name before the Lord in prayer. Ask Him to show you how you can speak 3B to each of them in the specific way they need to hear it. Ask God to give you sensitivity and discernment to their needs. Confess, repent, and commit to turn away from 3C speech and become a woman who only speaks one language: 3B, words that build, bless, and benefit

6. How has God spoken to your heart today?

reflect

Day Five

pray

1. How important is wisdom? Read today's proverb, and commit to seek and apply God's wisdom to your life as though your very life depended on it…because it does.

> *"Whoever finds me (wisdom) finds life and*
> *wins approval from the Lord.*
> *But those who miss me have injured themselves."*
> —Proverbs 8:35–36

I had a reality check at the mall one day. The cell phone of a woman who was shopping just a few feet away from me rang, and she answered it like this, "Where the _____ are you!!" I have no idea how the caller responded, but the woman's loud, profane rant continued for about a minute.

When she hung up, she stashed the phone back into her purse and went right back to her shopping—as though the phone had never rung. I was rattled by the reality of such a public explosion of profanity. But not her. She was less than three feet from me (she knew I had heard her) and she never said a single, "Sorry."

Now let me ask you a question: Who do you think was on the other end of that cell phone? Who do you think that Irritating Woman was talking to? People don't talk to their friends like that, do they? They wouldn't have any friends if they did. I think you and I both know who was on the other end of that cell phone. It was probably a member of that woman's own family – her husband or, perhaps, her child. It still sickens me when I think about that.

Too many teens are growing up in homes where words of death are spoken on a daily basis. How I pray that's not true of your home. But even if it is, precious girl, you cannot compromise or conform to the common standards of our culture. Your family members, friends, teachers—even the people who overhear your cell phone conversations and read your texts—should be the beneficiaries of your grace-filled words.

The principles you'll be learning from God's Word today will build on what you learned yesterday about 3B speech. As you embrace and apply these truths to your life, you'll not only build, bless, and benefit others, you'll become a powerful witness for Christ through your biblically beautiful speech.

2. Irritating Women tend to turn up the volume—and the attitude—when they speak. Read 1 Peter 3:1–4, and record what you learn about the spirit (attitude) and sound (volume) of a biblically beautiful girl.

3. Profanity, cursing, and cussing. You hear it everywhere: in conversations between girls (or guys) and their friends, in the lyrics of songs, on TV shows, and in movies. The culture doesn't seem to think there's anything profane about profanity, and even Christians are becoming more and more desensitized to it. But let's see what God's unchanging Word says about cussing and cursing. Read the following passage from James, and record what you learn about the tongue (the words you speak) and profanity:

James 3:6-12

> *6 And the tongue is a flame of fire. It is a whole world of wickedness, corrupting your entire body. It can set your whole life on fire, for it is set on fire by hell itself.*
>
> *7 People can tame all kinds of animals, birds, reptiles, and fish,*
>
> *8 but no one can tame the tongue. It is restless and evil, full of deadly poison.*
>
> *9 Sometimes it praises our Lord and Father, and sometimes it curses those who have been made in the image of God.*
>
> *10 And so blessing and cursing come pouring out of the same mouth. Surely, my brothers and sisters, this is not right!*
>
> *11 Does a spring of water bubble out with both fresh water and bitter water?*
>
> *12 Does a fig tree produce olives, or a grapevine produce figs? No, and you can't draw fresh water from a salty spring.*

4. I have a few super practical scriptures for you to look up. These verses contain some great "talking points"—wisdom and instructions to help you in your everyday conversation. Read each verse on the following chart, and briefly record the truth it teaches about talkin'.

Talking Points: Tips For Talkin'	
Proverbs 10:19	
Proverbs 15:4	
Proverbs 15:23, 25:11	
Proverbs 15:28	
Proverbs 17:14, 20:3	
Proverbs 17:27	

5. Before you do your weekly journal assignment, I want you to read one final scripture that was written just for you. After you read it, describe what God is saying specifically to you, a teenage girl, about your life and the words you speak.

Don't let anyone think less of you because you are young.
Be an example to all believers in what you say,
in the way you live, in your love, your faith, and your purity.
—1 Timothy 4:12

6. What has the Lord taught you this week, and how have you seen Him at work in your life? Journal your thoughts by completing the following sentence:

reflect

{ *This week the Lord...* _____

_____

_____

_____

More than any other single group of women on the planet, mothers-in-law rank number one on the Irritating Woman list—and I have officially joined their ranks. It was a role I felt some degree of dread about. I longed for a mother-in-law mentor—until I realized I already had one: my own precious mother-in-law, Frances Cole.

Fran is the model mother-in-law. She's supportive but not smothering. She's interested but not meddlesome. She's strong but not overbearing. And she's sweet, sweet, sweet. Although many miles separate us, and our times together are too far and few between, her welcome mat is always out and her smile outlasts our stay.

Annie Chapman wrote a wonderful book for mothers-in-law entitled *"The Mother-in-Law Dance."* In one chapter she refers to Proverbs 10:19 (one of the verses you just studied), and she says that for mothers-in-law, "Keeping our words to a minimum is one of the smartest ways to stay out of trouble. In fact, most any response that needs to be addressed can be summed up with three individual words. Those words are "sure," "really," and "wow."[10]

When Bill and I were 23 and our first son was a tiny baby, we bought a 40-foot travel trailer and went on the road in evangelism. We traveled from church to church and sang for revivals and evangelistic meetings. We lived on love offerings, and we trusted God to pay our bills and keep us fed. When I think about what I might do if one of my children did that today, I hope and pray I'd do just what Fran did—say, "Wow," and little else. Fran must have been worried about us…but we never knew it. Instead, she kept her concerns to herself and prayed for us often.

The term "mother-in-law" has historically been associated with adjectives like "aggravating," "troublemaking," "exasperating," and sometimes even "infuriating." But Frances Cole is a biblically beautiful woman who has shattered the stereotypical mother-in-law mold. And these days, I'm working very hard to follow in her footsteps.

Week Four • *How's That Irritating Woman Working for You?*

The Irritating Woman:

1. Outward signs: * _____, quarrelsome; hard to get along with
    * _____ and manipulating
    * _____, pleads and nags
    * demanding and _____

2. Inward issues: A desire to _____ and _____ others.

How's that Irritating Woman working for you?

1. _____ Story. It didn't work for her at all! *Num. 12:1–15*

2. _____ Story. It didn't work for her either! *2 Sam. 6:12–23*

What will work for you?

1. The Example of the Daughters of Zelophehad: *Num. 27:1–10*

    a. They took their _____ to those in _____.

    b. They stated their case _____, _____, and respectfully.

    c. They offered a simple, fair _____.

    d. They _____ the _____ to the authorities.

    RESULTS:
    They received what they needed *and* _____ _____, too.

2. The Example of _____ *Joshua 15:13–19*

3. Speaking _____: *Ephesians 4:29*

    a. A biblically beautiful young woman speaks _____ 3B.

    b. 3B words _____, _____, and _____ others.

Week 5 • *The Captivating Woman*

Can a biblically beautiful woman be sensual, sexual, and even seductive? Yes, BUT only if she's married. Proverbs describes a wife like this as "captivating," which means that she's the kind of wife whose husband is crazy in love with her. And if you get married someday, God wants you to be a Captivating Woman.

But what about now? Before you marry. Is it possible to be a Captivating Young Woman? Absolutely! Of course, that doesn't give you a green light to be sensual, sexual, or seductive (that's an Immoral Woman, remember), but you can become the kind of exceptional young woman that guys find very attractive.

This week, you'll discover the biblically beautiful qualities of the Captivating Young Woman. She's not a flirt. She's not a flatterer. And she's not a flaunter (as in itty-bitty shorts and bosom-baring shirts). But she can still attract a guy. And not just any guy. God's Guy. The kind of guy you'll definitely want to date and marry someday, which brings me to another topic you'll be studying this week: how to know if A Guy is God's Guy, or just another cutie-pie.

Precious girl, the principles you will learn this week are so important. Your decision to spend time studying God's Word is critical. So here's a little motivation to help you give this lesson your best effort yet. Every time you sit down to do your homework just think: one day your guy—God's Guy—will be so glad you did. And who knows? He might be a real cutie-pie, too.

Day One

1. Want to be prized, honored, and valued as a young woman? Then seek wisdom. Those who prize her will also be rewarded by her. Begin this week's lesson by praying and asking God to give you wisdom in every area of your life—including your dating and future married life.

> *If you prize wisdom, she will exalt you.*
> *Embrace her and she will honor you.*
> *She will place a lovely wreath on your head;*
> *she will present you with a beautiful crown.*
> —Proverbs 4:8–9

You met the **Captivating Woman** in your first week of this study. As you briefly renew your acquaintance with her today, remember: God included the Captivating Woman in His Word as a role model for your future relationship with your husband.

2. Read the beautiful description of the Captivating Woman:

> ¹⁸ *Let your wife be a fountain of blessing for you.*
> *Rejoice in the wife of your youth.*
> ¹⁹ *She is a loving doe, a graceful deer.*
> *Let her breasts satisfy you always.*
> *May you always be captivated by her love.*
> —Proverbs 5:18–19

Although you can't be a Captivating Woman until you get married, you can be the kind of girl that guys find fascinating, intriguing, and even get-down-on-one-knee-and-propose irresistible. Today you're going to meet a young woman just like that. Her name is Ruth, and if you want to learn how to become a biblically beautiful, stand-out-in-the-crowd Captivating Young Woman, Ruth's your role model. You're going to love getting to know her this week!

3. Meet Ruth by reading Ruth 1:1–18, 22. As you read, examine her character, her choices, and the decisions she makes.

Ruth 1:1-18, 22

> ¹ *In the days when the judges ruled in Israel, a severe famine came upon the land. So a man from Bethlehem in Judah left his home and went to live in the country of Moab, taking his wife and two sons with him.*
> ² *The man's name was Elimelech, and his wife was Naomi. Their two sons were Mahlon and Kilion. They were Ephrathites from Bethlehem in the land of Judah. And when they reached Moab, they settled there.*
> ³ *Then Elimelech died, and Naomi was left with her two sons.*
> ⁴ *The two sons married Moabite women. One married a woman named Orpah, and the other a woman named Ruth. But about ten years later,*
> ⁵ *both Mahlon and Kilion died. This left Naomi alone, without her two sons or her husband.*
> ⁶ *Then Naomi heard in Moab that the Lord had blessed his people in Judah by giving them good crops again. So Naomi and her daughters-in-law got ready to leave Moab to return to her homeland.*
> ⁷ *With her two daughters-in-law she set out from the place where she had been living, and they took the road that would lead them back to Judah.*
> ⁸ *But on the way, Naomi said to her two daughters-in-law, "Go back to your mothers' homes. And may the Lord reward you for your kindness to your husbands and to me.*

⁹ *May the Lord bless you with the security of another marriage." Then she kissed them good-bye, and they all broke down and wept.*

¹⁰ *"No," they said. "We want to go with you to your people."*

¹¹ *But Naomi replied, "Why should you go on with me? Can I still give birth to other sons who could grow up to be your husbands?*

¹² *No, my daughters, return to your parents' homes, for I am too old to marry again. And even if it were possible, and I were to get married tonight and bear sons, then what?*

¹³ *Would you wait for them to grow up and refuse to marry someone else? No, of course not, my daughters! Things are far more bitter for me than for you, because the Lord himself has raised his fist against me."*

¹⁴ *And again they wept together, and Orpah kissed her mother-in-law good-bye. But Ruth clung tightly to Naomi.*

¹⁵ *"Look," Naomi said to her, "your sister-in-law has gone back to her people and to her gods. You should do the same."*

¹⁶ *But Ruth replied, "Don't ask me to leave you and turn back. Wherever you go, I will go; wherever you live, I will live. Your people will be my people, and your God will be my God.*

¹⁷ *Wherever you die, I will die, and there I will be buried. May the Lord punish me severely if I allow anything but death to separate us!"*

¹⁸ *When Naomi saw that Ruth was determined to go with her, she said nothing more...*

²² *So Naomi returned from Moab, accompanied by her daughter-in-law Ruth, the young Moabite woman. They arrived in Bethlehem in late spring, at the beginning of the barley harvest.*

4. Record your answers to the following questions about Ruth:

   a. As a young woman, Ruth experienced an unexpected tragedy. What happened (verses 4–5)?

b.   Naomi, Ruth's mother-in-law, decided to leave Moab and return to her home in Bethlehem. Ruth and Orpah (Ruth's sister) went with Naomi as she started the journey, but what choice did Orpah ultimately make (v. 14–15)?

c.   What choices did Ruth make (verses 16–17)?

d.   Naomi warned Ruth repeatedly about the risks involved in her choices (verses 8–9, 11–13), yet Ruth accepted those risks and stuck with her decision. What does this reveal about Ruth and her character?

e.   What did Ruth's choices reveal about her faith and spirituality?

5.   I realize that you've only just met Ruth, but I wonder: What qualities does she possess that would make her a fantastic friend?

reflect

{

_____

_____

_____

_____

Day Two

pray

{

1. Take a few minutes to love yourself. How? By praying and asking God for wisdom as you study His Word today.

   To acquire wisdom is to love oneself;
   people who cherish understanding will prosper.
   —Proverbs 19:8

Yesterday, you read Ruth's "back story." She was born and raised in Moab, a land where idolatry and immorality were rampant. Both Ruth and her sister married into an Israelite family (a family that worshipped God) who had moved to Moab from Bethlehem because of a famine. Ruth must have grown to love and respect her new family very much, because when she, her sister, and her mother-in-law all became widows, she chose to move to Bethlehem with her mother-in-law, Naomi.

As a widow, Naomi had very little to offer Ruth, and when they arrived in Bethlehem, they were basically destitute. But it was the beginning of the barley harvest, and Israelite farmers were commanded by God to allow the poor to "glean"—to harvest the edges of the grain fields and to pick up and keep anything the workers dropped.

Today, you'll follow our girl, Ruth, to the harvest fields of Bethlehem where she will meet the man who will ultimately become the love of her life: Boaz. Watch Ruth carefully, and notice how she handles herself. There's so much you can learn from her. But be sure to study Boaz, too, girl, because he's just the kind of guy God's got in mind for you.

2. Get to know Ruth better as you read Ruth 2.

Ruth 2

¹ *Now there was a wealthy and influential man in Bethlehem named Boaz, who was a relative of Naomi's husband, Elimelech.*

² *One day Ruth the Moabite said to Naomi, "Let me go out into the harvest fields to pick up the stalks of grain left behind by anyone who is kind enough to let me do it." Naomi replied, "All right, my daughter, go ahead."*

³ *So Ruth went out to gather grain behind the harvesters. And as it happened, she found herself working in a field that belonged to Boaz, the relative of her father-in-law, Elimelech.*

⁴ *While she was there, Boaz arrived from Bethlehem and greeted the harvesters. "The Lord be with you!" he said. "The Lord bless you!" the harvesters replied.*

⁵ *Then Boaz asked his foreman, "Who is that young woman over there? Who does she belong to?"*

⁶ *And the foreman replied, "She is the young woman from Moab who came back with Naomi.*

⁷ *She asked me this morning if she could gather grain behind the harvesters. She has been hard at work ever since, except for a few minutes' rest in the shelter."*

⁸ *Boaz went over and said to Ruth, "Listen, my daughter. Stay right here with us when you gather grain; don't go to any other fields. Stay right behind the young women working in my field.*

⁹ *See which part of the field they are harvesting, and then follow them. I have warned the young men not to treat you roughly. And when you are thirsty, help yourself to the water they have drawn from the well."*

¹⁰ *Ruth fell at his feet and thanked him warmly. "What have I done to deserve such kindness?" she asked. "I am only a foreigner."*

¹¹ *"Yes, I know," Boaz replied. "But I also know about everything you have done for your mother-in-law since the death of your husband. I have heard how you left your father and mother and your own land to live here among complete strangers.*

¹² *May the Lord, the God of Israel, under whose wings you have come to take refuge, reward you fully for what you have done."*

¹³ *"I hope I continue to please you, sir," she replied. "You have comforted me by speaking so kindly to me, even though I am not one of your workers."*

¹⁴ *At mealtime Boaz called to her, "Come over here, and help yourself to some food. You can dip your bread in the sour wine." So she sat with his harvesters, and Boaz gave her some roasted grain to eat. She ate all she wanted and still had some left over.*

¹⁵ *When Ruth went back to work again, Boaz ordered his young men, "Let her gather grain right among the sheaves without stopping her.*

¹⁶ *And pull out some heads of barley from the bundles and drop them on purpose for her. Let her pick them up, and don't give her a hard time!"*

¹⁷ *So Ruth gathered barley there all day, and when she beat out the grain that evening, it filled an entire basket.*

¹⁸ *She carried it back into town and showed it to her mother-in-law. Ruth also gave her the roasted grain that was left over from her meal.*

¹⁹ *"Where did you gather all this grain today?" Naomi asked. "Where did you work? May the Lord bless the one who helped you!" So Ruth told her mother-in-law about the man in whose field she had worked. She said, "The man I worked with today is named Boaz."*

²⁰ *"May the Lord bless him!" Naomi told her daughter-in-law. "He is showing his kindness to us as well as to your dead husband. That man is one of our closest relatives, one of our family redeemers."*

²¹ *Then Ruth said, "What's more, Boaz even told me to come back and stay with his harvesters until the entire harvest is completed."*

²² *"Good!" Naomi exclaimed. "Do as he said, my daughter. Stay with his young women right through the whole harvest. You might be harassed in other fields, but you'll be safe with him."*

²³ *So Ruth worked alongside the women in Boaz's fields and gathered grain with them until the end of the barley harvest. Then she continued working with them through the wheat harvest in early summer. And all the while she lived with her mother-in-law.*

3. Record your answers to the following questions:

   a. How did Ruth end up in Boaz's field (verses 2-3)? Did she know who he was and purposefully go to his field on a husband-hunting expedition?

   b. According to the foreman, what did Ruth do all morning (verse 7), and what does this reveal about her?

c. How did Ruth meet Boaz? Who made the first move (verse 8), and what does this reveal about Ruth?

d. How did Ruth handle herself around Boaz (verses 10 & 13)? Was she a flirt?

e. What kind of reputation did Ruth have (verses 11–12)?

f. What specific things did Boaz do to protect and provide for Ruth (verses 8–9, 14–16, 21)?

4. In what way is Boaz like the kind of guy you'd like to date or marry (and don't include "rich" ☺)?

reflect

_____

_____

_____

_____

Day Three

pray

1. According to today's Proverb, getting wisdom is a priority. Pray and ask God to give you wisdom as you continue to study Ruth and Boaz. Commit to take what He's taught you through their example, and apply it to your life today.

Getting wisdom is the most important thing you can do!
—Proverbs 4:7

We can't know for sure whether or not sparks flew when Ruth and Boaz met, but they certainly seemed to admire one another. Boaz showed his admiration by the affirming words he spoke to Ruth, and Ruth showed her admiration for him by responding to him with honor and respect. I'd say their relationship was off to a really good start, wouldn't you?

Weeks went by as Ruth continued to glean in Boaz's fields, and this gave them the opportunity to observe and get to know one another better. But dating? No, they didn't really date back then. So how will our two lovebirds ever get together? Find out today as the harvest season ends and their commitment to one another begins.

2. Read Ruth 3, an exciting turning point in the story and saga of Ruth.

Ruth 3

¹ One day Naomi said to Ruth, "My daughter, it's time that I found a permanent home for you, so that you will be provided for.

² Boaz is a close relative of ours, and he's been very kind by letting you gather grain with his young women. Tonight he will be winnowing barley at the threshing floor.

³ Now do as I tell you—take a bath and put on perfume and dress in your nicest clothes. Then go to the threshing floor, but don't let Boaz see you until he has finished eating and drinking.

⁴ Be sure to notice where he lies down; then go and uncover his feet and lie down there. He will tell you what to do."

⁵ "I will do everything you say," Ruth replied.

⁶ So she went down to the threshing floor that night and followed the instructions of her mother-in-law.

⁷ After Boaz had finished eating and drinking and was in good spirits, he lay down at the far end of the pile of grain and went to sleep. Then Ruth came quietly, uncovered his feet, and lay down.

⁸ Around midnight Boaz suddenly woke up and turned over. He was surprised to find a woman lying at his feet!

⁹ "Who are you?" he asked. "I am your servant Ruth," she replied. "Spread the corner of your covering over me, for you are my family redeemer."

¹⁰ "The Lord bless you, my daughter!" Boaz exclaimed. "You are showing even more family loyalty now than you did before, for you have not gone after a younger man, whether rich or poor.

¹¹ Now don't worry about a thing, my daughter. I will do what is necessary, for everyone in town knows you are a virtuous woman.

¹² But while it's true that I am one of your family redeemers, there is another man who is more closely related to you than I am.

¹³ Stay here tonight, and in the morning I will talk to him. If he is willing to redeem you, very well. Let him marry you. But if he is not willing, then as surely as the Lord lives, I will redeem you myself! Now lie down here until morning."

¹⁴ So Ruth lay at Boaz's feet until the morning, but she got up before it was light enough for people to recognize each other. For Boaz had said, "No one must know that a woman was here at the threshing floor."

¹⁵ Then Boaz said to her, "Bring your cloak and spread it out." He measured six scoops of barley into the cloak and placed it on her back. Then he returned to the town.

¹⁶ When Ruth went back to her mother-in-law, Naomi asked, "What happened, my daughter?" Ruth told Naomi everything Boaz had done for her,

¹⁷ and she added, "He gave me these six scoops of barley and said, 'Don't go back to your mother-in-law empty-handed.'"

¹⁸ Then Naomi said to her, "Just be patient, my daughter, until we hear what happens. The man won't rest until he has settled things today."

3. Record your answers to the following questions:

   a. What did Naomi tell Ruth to do and why (verses 1–4)?

   b. Did Ruth do as Naomi told her? Circle the correct answer:

      Yes   No

   c. If you had been Ruth, would you have followed Naomi's instructions? Circle one of the following answers:

      No, absolutely not!   Yes, you betcha!   Yikes! I'm not sure

   Naomi's instructions to Ruth seem really strange, I know. But keep in mind that Naomi loved Ruth and wanted the very best for her. Plus, she knew that Boaz could redeem Ruth, which meant that he had the legal right to purchase the land that belonged to Elimelech and his sons (Naomi's deceased husband and sons) and marry Ruth.

   You may also be wondering why Naomi told Ruth to lie down at Boaz's feet as he slept. Well, according to the customs of that day, by lying at his feet and requesting that Boaz cover her with his garment, Ruth was symbolically asking him to protect her by becoming her redeemer and husband.

   It took a lot of faith and courage for Ruth to follow Naomi's instructions. But I think Naomi knew by the way Boaz treated Ruth that he loved her. Plus, Ruth and Naomi were tight. She must have been aware of Ruth's love for Boaz. Sensing that the time was ripe for a commitment, and wanting the very best for her beloved Ruth, God used Naomi to bring Ruth and Boaz together.

Now I want you to consider another very important issue that relates to Ruth Chapter 3. Some guys will tell a girl that they love them—and maybe even want to marry them someday—when all they really want is sex. And some girls will go to bed or even move in with a guy like that. So how can you really know if a guy truly loves you or if he just wants to have sex with you? To answer to that question, let's examine Ruth 3:13–14 again.

4. Read Ruth 3:13–14, and notice the verbal commitment Boaz made to Ruth. How did Ruth know that his words were sincere and that he wasn't just attempting to get her to have sex with him? (verse 14)?

5. How can you know if a guy really loves you or if you love him? In other words, how can you recognize a love that is true? Read 1 Corinthians 13:4–8, and record what you learn about love by completing the following sentence:

    A guy who really loves me will be _____

    _____

    _____

    _____

6. What have you learned today to help you know whether or not a guy is sincere in his love and commitment to you…and you to him?

reflect {

    _____

    _____

    _____

    _____

Day Four

1. Begin your time of study today by praying and asking God to use the wisdom He is giving you this week to guard and protect your future.

Don't turn your back on wisdom, for she will protect you.
Love her, and she will guard you.
—Proverbs 4:6

I hope the real-life love story of Ruth and Boaz has inspired and encouraged you this week. But most of all, I hope you know that God cares for you every bit as much as He cared for Ruth. He has incredible plans for you, so do not settle for anything less than His best as you date and, perhaps, marry.

When Ruth made the choice to leave her old life behind and follow Naomi and God by faith, she probably never dreamed God had such amazing plans in store for her. Precious girl, be a modern-day Ruth. Follow God and His path for your life no matter what the risks or costs may be. And as you read the happy ending of Ruth's story today, know this: God promises to reward all—and that includes you—who seek Him (Hebrews 11:6).

2. Read Ruth 4:1–13.

Ruth 4:1-13

¹ *Boaz went to the town gate and took a seat there. Just then the family redeemer he had mentioned came by, so Boaz called out to him, "Come over here and sit down, friend. I want to talk to you." So they sat down together.*

² *Then Boaz called ten leaders from the town and asked them to sit as witnesses.*

³ *And Boaz said to the family redeemer, "You know Naomi, who came back from Moab. She is selling the land that belonged to our relative Elimelech.*

⁴ *I thought I should speak to you about it so that you can redeem it if you wish. If you want the land, then buy it here in the presence of these witnesses. But if you don't want it, let me know right away, because I am next in line to redeem it after you." The man replied, "All right, I'll redeem it."*

⁵ Then Boaz told him, "Of course, your purchase of the land from Naomi also requires that you marry Ruth, the Moabite widow. That way she can have children who will carry on her husband's name and keep the land in the family."

⁶ "Then I can't redeem it," the family redeemer replied, "because this might endanger my own estate. You redeem the land; I cannot do it."

⁷ Now in those days it was the custom in Israel for anyone transferring a right of purchase to remove his sandal and hand it to the other party. This publicly validated the transaction.

⁸ So the other family redeemer drew off his sandal as he said to Boaz, "You buy the land."

⁹ Then Boaz said to the elders and to the crowd standing around, "You are witnesses that today I have bought from Naomi all the property of Elimelech, Kilion, and Mahlon.

¹⁰ And with the land I have acquired Ruth, the Moabite widow of Mahlon, to be my wife. This way she can have a son to carry on the family name of her dead husband and to inherit the family property here in his hometown. You are all witnesses today."

¹¹ Then the elders and all the people standing in the gate replied, "We are witnesses! May the Lord make this woman who is coming into your home like Rachel and Leah, from whom all the nation of Israel descended! May you prosper in Ephrathah and be famous in Bethlehem.

¹² And may the Lord give you descendants by this young woman who will be like those of our ancestor Perez, the son of Tamar and Judah."

¹³ So Boaz took Ruth into his home, and she became his wife. When he slept with her, the Lord enabled her to become pregnant, and she gave birth to a son.

3. Record your answers to the following questions:

   a. In Ruth 3:13, Boaz promised Ruth that he would do everything within his power to redeem and marry her. According to what you just read, how did Boaz fulfill his promise (verses 1–8)?

   b. Put yourself in Ruth's shoes. How do you think she felt when she heard about the way Boaz had publicly proclaimed his desire and intention to marry her?

   c. How did God bless Ruth and Boaz (verse 13)?

4. Think back to the first chapter of Ruth and the way Ruth's story begins. Now fast forward to Ruth 4 and the way Ruth's story ends. As you consider these two very different chapters of the same book, answer the following questions:

   a. What did you learn about the importance of making good choices even when it's hard and it seems risky?

   b. Why do you think God recorded the beautiful love story of Ruth and Boaz in the Bible? What is He saying to you today?

5. What characteristic in Ruth's life do you most desire in yours? Explain your answer.

reflect {

_____

_____

_____

_____

Day Five

pray {

1. Embracing the culture's beliefs (or even our own personal opinions) about dating, sex, and marriage is very dangerous. Before you begin your final day of study this week, spend a few minutes in prayer. Commit to embrace the wisdom and truth God has shown you through your study of Ruth.

Trusting oneself is foolish, but those who walk in wisdom are safe.
—Proverbs 28:26

Today you will discover God's #1 requirement for any guy you date. It is the most important quality you should look for in any potential date. Why? Because A Guy you date will eventually become The Guy you marry. But before you find out what God's #1 requirement is, spend a few minutes reflecting upon the story of Ruth and Boaz.

2. Recall and review the story of Ruth and Boaz. As you picture each chapter in your mind, record on the following chart several reasons why you think Ruth and Boaz were attracted to one another.

I think Ruth was attracted to Boaz because…	I think Boaz was attracted to Ruth because…

Precious girl, I hope your study of Ruth will enable you to recognize a Boaz, the kind of guy God has in mind for you. Yes, he is rare, but he's out there, so be patient. Follow God (like Ruth did), and if His plans for your life include marriage, He'll lead you to your Boaz. And never ever settle for a Bozo!

Bozo is the counterfeit version (evil twin) of Boaz. Unlike Boaz, Bozo won't protect you (or your purity), and he won't provide for you either. That's because Bozo is a taker, not a giver. He's also a talker—as in "sweet talker." Honey, Bozo will promise you the moon, but he's all talk and no commitment. Do not waste your time, and do not give your heart to Bozo— he'll just take it and break it.

One of the primary ways you can know whether or not a guy is a Boaz or a Bozo is by making sure he meets God's #1 requirement for any guy that you date. Discover that essential, foremost requirement right now.

3. Read 2 Corinthians 6:14 (I'm giving it to you in two translations), and record in your own words God's #1 requirement for any guy that you date.

2 Corinthians 6:14 *(NIV)*

Do not be yoked together with unbelievers.
For what do righteousness and wickedness have in common?
Or what fellowship can light have with darkness?

2 Corinthians 6:14

Don't team up with those who are unbelievers.
How can righteousness be a partner with wickedness?
How can light live with darkness?

God's #1 requirement for any guy that I date is:

So, how can you know if a guy meets this requirement? Well, before you go out with him, you're going to have to talk to him and ask him some very important questions like, "What do you believe about God, Jesus, and the Bible?" And you absolutely have to ask him, "Are you a Christian?" If he's wishy-washy, or if his answers are unbiblical, then you know you can't "team up" with him. To be succinct, you cannot date him (and if you do, you'll be making a choice that is in direct disobedience to God—a dangerous thing to do).

But even if he answers every question correctly and tells you that he's a Christian, there's still one more thing you need to do before you can go out with him…and you're about to find out what that is.

4. Read Matthew 7:16–23 and Galatians 5:22–23, then answer the questions that follow.

Matthew 7:16–23

You can identify [people] by their fruit, that is, by the way they act. Can you pick grapes from thornbushes, or figs from thistles? A good tree produces good fruit, and a bad tree produces bad fruit. A good tree can't produce bad fruit, and a bad tree can't produce good fruit…Yes, just as you can identify a tree by its fruit, so you can identify people by their actions. Not everyone who calls out to me, "Lord! Lord!" will enter the Kingdom of Heaven. Only those who actually do the will of my Father in heaven will enter. On judgment day many will say to me, "Lord! Lord! We prophesied in your name and cast out demons in your name and performed many miracles in your name." But I will reply, "I never knew you. Get away from me, you who break God's laws."

Galatians 5:22–23

But the Holy Spirit produces this kind of fruit in our lives: love, joy, peace, patience, kindness, goodness, faithfulness, gentleness, and self-control.

a. According to Matthew 7:16–21, how can you identify what kind of person somebody is?

b. According to Galatians 5:22–23, how can you know if a guy (or anyone else) is a Christian?

c.   So, before you "team up" and date (or marry) a guy, what should you do?

5.   What kind of guy do you want to say, "I do," to? What traits and characteristics do you want him to possess? Consider these questions and everything you've learned this week, then make a list of these qualities by completing the following sentence:

If I ever get married, I want my husband to be...

I want to encourage you to make a copy of that list, and keep it somewhere handy. Use it often as you pray asking God to build each specific characteristic into your future husband's heart and life. And as you prepare to date, you can also use your list as a standard to help guide you to God's guy.

6. How has the Lord encouraged and spoken to your heart this week? What specific actions is He leading you to take in response to what He's taught you? Conclude your week of study by taking a couple of minutes to journal your answers to these questions.

reflect

This week the Lord... _____

_____

_____

_____

She was a beautiful little girl when she learned a very ugly truth: some men are predators, not protectors. Used and abused, she longed to be loved. But in her pursuit for love, she became a statistic instead: a pregnant teen.

A few years later, she moved to Houston seeking a new start. Soon, she met a man who vowed to love, honor, and cherish her. But unfaithfulness tore their marriage apart, and she was left with two small children and no one to protect and provide for her or them.

With a pain-filled past and a frightening future before her, she sought love from the only One she had left: God. And He lavished His love upon her. He taught her what true love really is. He became her Protector and her Provider. And as her confidence and security in His love for her grew, He even healed the wounds from her childhood.

I met her at church. Her name was Christy, and we became friends. Her love for God and hunger to grow in His Word was stunning. As I got to know her and her two little boys, I became an eyewitness to the miraculous way that God can be a Husband to the husbandless and a Father to the fatherless.

Christy remained a single mom for several years. But one day, after reading the Book of Ruth, she whispered a bold, brief prayer: "Lord, I know You can do for me what You did for Ruth. Please, God, bring me a Boaz." And He did! Now my beloved friend, Christy, is the captivating wife of David Simmons, a loving, giving, godly man.

Precious girl, be a Ruth. Be a Christy. Pursue God, not guys, because that's what will transform and enable you to become a Captivating Young Woman. Then don't be surprised when God brings a Boaz your way. He delights in doing things like that for girls like Ruth. And Christy. And you.

Week Five • *How a Godly Girl Attracts a Godly Guy*

<u>Step 1</u>: **Embrace God's _____ as your _____;
only date / marry a Christian.**

*"Don't team up with those who are unbelievers. How can righteousness
be a partner with wickedness? How can light live with darkness?"*
—2 Corinthians 6:14 NLT

<u>Step 2</u>: **Follow Ruth's example; become a _____
young woman.**

1) Give God _____ in your life. *Ruth 1:16, Psalm 37:3-6*

2) _____ the _____ of others by:
   * your virtuous _____ *Ruth 2:10-13, Psalm 37:6*
   * your willingness to _____ *Ruth 2:2-3, 6-7*

3) Take care of your _____ _____.
   Ruth 3:3

4) Do not compromise your _____ _____.
   Ruth 2-3

5) Let your desire for a _____ to _____
   be known. *Ruth 3:6-9*

<u>Step 3</u>: **Learn to _____ a godly guy.**

1) He will give God _____ in his life. *Ruth 2:4, 8-15*

2) He will be _____ by others.

3) He will _____ you. *Ruth 2:8, 15*

4) He will _____ for you. *Ruth 2:8-9, 14-16*

5) He will make a _____ to you and will
   _____ follow through with it. *Ruth 3:11-4:10*

Week 6 • *The Ideal Woman*

Dessert has always been my favorite course—even if it's just a couple of Oreos after a peanut butter and banana sandwich. Some say, "Life's short—eat dessert first." But not me. I like saving the best for last. And that's exactly how I feel about this final lesson on Beauty Do #2, the Ideal Woman. Of all the women presented in Proverbs, she's the best, so she is saved as the final and most satisfying course.

Now don't get the wrong idea. The Ideal Woman is no fancy cream puff or sugar-filled bonbon. She's a woman of substance. She leads a purposeful and significant life. Although she wears many hats and juggles numerous responsibilities, she balances the various aspects of her life with wisdom, integrity, and lots of love. Girl, she's the kind of woman God wants you to become.

While I was writing the first *Beauty by The Book* study (the one for adult women), one of my favorite friends called to encourage me. She said, "I really like that you used the word 'becoming' in the subtitle of the study—I like that word. It reminds me that biblical beauty is a process." To be honest, I hadn't even considered that, but I was so grateful God revealed it to her and led her to share it with me.

Biblical beauty is, indeed, a process. So don't be intimidated by the **Ideal Woman** this week—even she had to go through the process of "becoming." And if she made it, girl, you can, too. Here's to "becoming."

Day One

1. If you're a sugar addict like I am, you're going to love today's proverb! Read it, then pray and ask God to make this week's lesson a sweet treat and a delicious dessert of wisdom from His Word.

> *My child, eat honey, for it is good,*
> *and the honeycomb is sweet to the taste.*
> *In the same way, wisdom is sweet to your soul.*
> *If you find it, you will have a bright future,*
> *and your hopes will not be cut short.*
> —Proverbs 24:13–14

As I was preparing this final lesson of our study and thinking about you, the Lord brought a specific passage to my heart. Take a look:

> *Older women must train the younger women to love their husbands and*
> *their children, to live wisely and be pure, to work in their homes,*
> *to do good, and to be submissive to their husbands.*
> *Then they will not bring shame on the word of God.*
> —Titus 2:4–5

Titus 2:4-5 instructs older women, like me, to train younger women, like you. It even includes a list of the specific things I'm supposed to teach you: to love your future husband and children, to live wisely and be pure, to work in your home, and to do good (yes, it also includes teaching you to be submissive to your own husband, but since we studied that in Week 4, we won't cover that topic this week). And I'm very excited because the woman we will be studying this week—the Ideal Woman—embodies everything in that list.

Before we begin our Titus 2 training, I want you to know that even if you never marry, you can (and should) become an Ideal Woman. Why? Because she is a role model for all women young and old, single and married. Although I will be using the Ideal Woman to teach you the Titus 2 curriculum and prepare you for marriage and a family someday, the strengths and characteristics of the Ideal Woman will apply to your life today and to your future whether or not you marry. So with that said, let's begin our Titus 2 training by studying a biblical beauty par excellence: the Ideal Woman

2. Find out about the Ideal Woman and her husband by reading the following scriptures from Proverbs 31:

    Who can find a virtuous and capable wife?
    She is worth more than precious rubies. Her husband can trust her,
    and she will greatly enrich his life.
    She will not hinder him but help him all of her life.
    —Proverbs 31:10–12

    Her husband is well known, for he sits
    in the council meeting with the other civic leaders.
    —Proverbs 31:23

    Her husband praises her: "There are many virtuous and
    capable women in the world, but you surpass them all!"
    —Proverbs 31:28b-29

3. The very first characteristic you learn about the Ideal Woman is that she's trustworthy. Think about that as you answer the following questions:

    a. What's so important about being trustworthy? Is it essential for a strong relationship? Why or why not?

b. Why is trust especially important between a husband and wife?

c. When you marry, what are some things you can do to earn your husband's trust? For example, you could choose not to text, call, or chat online with any of your former boyfriends. Excluding those examples, what other things can you do (or maybe not do) to earn your husband's trust?

d. Are you trustworthy? What can you do today to become a young woman that others trust?

4. The Ideal Woman helps her husband and enriches his life (verses 10–12). Record some practical ways a wife can help her husband and enrich his life.

5. Although the word "love" is never used in the verses you just read from Proverbs 31, how do you know that the Ideal Woman loves her husband?

6. What are some non-verbal ways you can communicate your love to your family and friends today?

reflect {

_____

_____

_____

_____

Day Two

pray {

1. Wisdom enables us to build our homes and to build up the people we love. Ask God to give you wisdom to build the home and family you live with today, and the home you may share with your future husband and children someday.

A wise woman builds her home, but a foolish woman tears it down with her own hands.
—Proverbs 14:1

Yesterday we began our Titus 2 older woman/younger woman training session, and you learned how to love your future husband. Today's lesson will teach you some very practical ways you can love your future children.

Your role model this week is our fifth and final female from Proverbs: The Ideal Woman. As you study her relationship with her kids, I'm praying that she will inspire you to become a mom just like her someday.

2. Find out about the Ideal Woman and her responsibilities and relationship with her children by reading the following verses:

> *She gets up before dawn to prepare breakfast for her household.*
> —Proverbs 31:15

> *She has no fear of winter for her household,*
> *for everyone has warm clothes.*
> —Proverbs 31:21

> *When she speaks, her words are wise,*
> *and she gives instructions with kindness.*
> *She carefully watches everything in her household*
> *and suffers nothing from laziness.*
> *Her children stand and bless her.*
> —Proverbs 31:26–28

3. According to Proverbs 31:15, 21, 26-28, what are some of the specific ways the Ideal Woman takes care of her children?

4. Has God placed any children (younger brothers, sisters, cousins, children you babysit, etc.) in your life? If so, how can you care for them like an Ideal Woman would?

5. Think about the time, money, work, etc. involved in taking care of children. Now think about the number of years in her life that a mom spends caring for her kids. With all of that in mind, what specific skills and character qualities will it take for you to care for your future children like the Ideal Woman does?

6. According to Proverbs 31:26-28, how does the Ideal Woman motivate and communicate with her children? How do they feel about her?

As a mom, I can tell you that receiving a compliment from one of my children means more than almost anything in the world to me. A hug and a kind word from one of my sons can make my spirit soar even on the worst of days. I'm pretty sure your mom feels the very same way.

Girl, have you blessed your mom today? Have you praised or complimented her lately? Let the Lord use you in a HUGE way today. Put your arms around your mom, and say something sweet to her. It'll make you feel good, too.

7. When your future children are grown, what do you want them to remember about you and the kind of mom that you were? What do you hope they'll tell your future grandkids about you?

reflect

_____

_____

_____

_____

Day Three

pray

1. Wisdom + good sense = a strong house. Today, ask God to give you both wisdom and good sense.

    A house is built by wisdom and
    becomes strong through good sense.
    —Proverbs 24:3

Take a look at the very first verse that describes the Ideal Woman:

Who can find a virtuous and capable wife?
—Proverbs 31:10

Notice the first adjective used to describe her. It's the word "virtuous." To some people, this word conjures up a picture of someone who is way too perfect and has absolutely no fun whatsoever. But that's not what "virtuous" means at all. What it actually means is strength, influence, and character.[11]

In Titus 2:4–5, older women are commanded to train younger women to be wise, pure, and to do good to others. The Ideal Woman in Proverbs 31 exemplifies all of these virtues and more. And although you are young, you can possess these virtues, too (I Timothy 4:12).

As you study the Ideal Woman's character today, I want you to "try on" some of the adjectives Proverbs 31 uses to describe her. And trust me—they'll fit. That's one of my favorite things about God's Word. Every verse is one-size-fits-all. Makes "becoming" an Ideal Woman seem very doable!

2. Read and reread Proverbs 31:10–31, and circle the words that describe the Ideal Woman's character and strengths. Also, as you notice specific qualities that you admire about her, record your personal impressions and notes in the margins. Take your time on this. Do not rush.

Proverbs 31:10–31

10 *Who can find a virtuous and capable wife? She is more precious than rubies.*

11 *Her husband can trust her, and she will greatly enrich his life.*

12 *She brings him good, not harm, all the days of her life.*

13 *She finds wool and flax and busily spins it.*

14 *She is like a merchant's ship, bringing her food from afar.*

15 *She gets up before dawn to prepare breakfast for her household and plan the day's work for her servant girls.*

16 *She goes to inspect a field and buys it; with her earnings she plants a vineyard.*

17 *She is energetic and strong, a hard worker.*

18 *She makes sure her dealings are profitable; her lamp burns late into the night.*

19 *Her hands are busy spinning thread, her fingers twisting fiber.*

20 *She extends a helping hand to the poor and opens her arms to the needy.*

21 *She has no fear of winter for her household, for everyone has warm clothes.*

22 *She makes her own bedspreads. She dresses in fine linen and purple gowns.*

23 *Her husband is well known at the city gates, where he sits with the other civic leaders.*

24 *She makes belted linen garments and sashes to sell to the merchants.*

25 *She is clothed with strength and dignity, and she laughs without fear of the future.*

26 *When she speaks, her words are wise, and she gives instructions with kindness.*

27 *She carefully watches everything in her household and suffers nothing from laziness.*

28 *Her children stand and bless her. Her husband praises her:*

29 *"There are many virtuous and capable women in the world, but you surpass them all!"*

30 *Charm is deceptive, and beauty does not last; but a woman who fears the Lord will be greatly praised.*

31 *Reward her for all she has done. Let her deeds publicly declare her praise.*

---

3. Record the top three qualities (virtues) you admire about the Ideal Woman.

    # 1 _____

    # 2 _____

    # 3 _____

4. Now, "try on" the top three qualities you selected by completing the following sentences:

    # 1 I can put on this quality by _____

    _____

    # 2 I can put on this quality by _____

    _____

    # 3 I can put on this quality by _____

    _____

5. What would your best friend say are your two best character qualities?

6. What would you say are your two weakest character qualities, and what can you do to strengthen them?

reflect {

_____

_____

_____

_____

Day Four

pray

1. Before you begin today's lesson, thank God for the wise women He's placed in your life. Ask Him to grow and mature you in wisdom so that you will become a wise woman for others to follow.

    Wisdom is enshrined in an understanding heart;
    wisdom is not found among fools.

    —Proverbs 14:33

The Ideal Woman is one hard-working gal. It's just one more way that she epitomizes Titus 2:4–5, "Older women must train the younger women…to work in their homes." Although housework may not be the most glamorous thing in the world, our homes and the way we care for them should reflect biblical beauty.

Someday, you'll have your own home to care for, so the first part of today's lesson will focus on the home management skills of the Ideal Woman. Welcome to one of the most down-to-earth, practical parts of our study on biblical beauty: Housework 101.

2. Using the Proverbs 31 passage in yesterday's lesson, compile a list of the responsibilities the Ideal Woman oversees and performs for her home and household.

    NOTE: Don't include her business/job responsibilities. We'll study that aspect of her work in a few minutes.

Homekeeping Responsibilities	

3. How are your homekeeping skills? What can you do today to help around your home and to prepare to keep your own home someday?

You probably noticed that the Ideal Woman had "servant girls" (plural even) to help her. So maybe you're thinking, "When I have a house someday, I'm going to hire a maid or two to help me, too." Hey, if you can afford to hire some help, that's great.

But if you have children in that home you own someday, you need to train them to help and serve around the house (whether you have a maid or not). I used to fuss, mope, and literally seethe at my mother for making me do chores around the house, but now I'm so glad she was unfazed by my pouting. Mother held her ground, made me work, and never let me get by with a second-rate effort—I couldn't "clock out" until I passed her inspection. Because of her strength and fortitude, she managed to teach me (a very unwilling student) how to keep a proper house.

Is housework the Ideal Woman's only work, or does she also work outside the home? And what does God's Word say about wives and moms working outside the home? Find the answers to these questions as you finish today's lesson.

4. Using the Proverbs 31 passage in yesterday's homework, answer the following questions:

    a. Does the Ideal Woman work outside the home? Circle your answer.

        Yes   No

    b. Record the specific verses from the Proverbs 31 passage that you based your answer upon.

5. Earlier this week, you learned how the Ideal Woman takes care of her husband and children. Today you've studied her work inside and outside the home. With everyone she has to take care of and with everything she has to do, how do you think she balances it all? What scriptural evidence do you see in Proverbs 31 about the priorities of the Ideal Woman?

6. How did the Ideal Woman's income impact her family and others? What did you learn about the way she manages her finances?

7. As you think about your future family, home, and work, what will your priorities be? How will you balance family, home, and career?

reflect

Day Five

pray

1. For the past six weeks, you've been praying for wisdom using scriptures from the Old Testament Book of Proverbs. But today's scripture is different. It's from the New Testament, and it's a direct quote from the lips of Christ about *wisdom*. A wise young woman's life is a witness to others that God's way—the way of wisdom—is the right way. Praise and thank Him today for the wisdom He's given to you, and ask Him to use your life to point others to Him.

> *But wisdom is shown to be right by the lives of those who follow it.*
> —Luke 7:35

It's our final day of study together. We made it to the finish line! I hope you've enjoyed getting to know the five females from the Proverbs as much as I have. But more than that, I hope you've learned what it takes to become a true beauty—a biblical beauty.

Your study will be light today. I want to give you some extra time to reflect back over the past six weeks and praise the Father for all that He's taught you. Thank you, thank you, precious girl, for your hunger for God's Word and for your commitment to spend time studying it with me. May you enjoy and experience the pleasure of His presence as you meet with Him today.

2. Read Proverbs 31:30–31, and answer the following questions:

a. The covers of fashion magazines, the experts on infomercials, and the celebs and beauty gurus everywhere all promise the same thing: the secrets of true beauty. They offer potions, programs, and products galore guaranteed to make you beautiful. But what's the real truth about beauty (v. 30)?

b.   What is the "secret" to biblical beauty (verse 30b)?

c.   What is the "payoff" for biblical beauty (verses 30b–31)?

3.   As your final assignment in this study, take time to praise and thank God for the primary principles He's taught you over the past six weeks. Flip slowly through each lesson in this workbook, and review how He spoke to you through the Immoral Woman, the Indiscreet Woman, the Irritating Woman, the Captivating Woman, and the Ideal Woman. As you review each lesson, complete the following prayer that corresponds with it. Let this be a sweet time of fellowship and overflowing praise to the Lord.

Father, thank you for speaking to me as I studied the Immoral Woman.
I praise and thank you for specifically showing me...

Father, thank you for speaking to me as I studied the Indiscreet Woman.
I praise and thank you for specifically showing me…

Father, thank you for speaking to me as I studied the Irritating Woman.
I praise and thank you for specifically showing me…

Father, thank you for speaking to me as I studied the Captivating Woman.
I praise and thank you for specifically showing me…

Father, thank you for speaking to me as I studied the Ideal Woman.
I praise and thank you for specifically showing me…

At the conclusion of each lesson, I've shared some real-life biblical beauties with you. But just like the Book of Proverbs, I've saved the best for last.

You see, I was raised by an Ideal Woman. Her name is Julia McKay. Virtuous, industrious, energetic and strong, she raised me and my four brothers mostly by herself. I'm sure Mother grew weary as she shouldered the load of raising a large family while Daddy traveled as an evangelist—but she did it. Day by day, she just did it.

And while she did it, she cooked and cleaned, did the laundry and ironed, shopped and kept the pantry filled (an almost impossible task with four boys), oversaw our homework and read to us, got us to church almost every time the doors were open, worked in the yard and gardened, all the while chauffeuring us to piano lessons, football practice, and baseball games.

But it wasn't until I got older that I realized the most important thing Mother had done for us: "She (opened) her mouth in wisdom, and the teaching of kindness (was) on her tongue" (Proverbs 31:26 *NASB*). Somehow in the midst of those crazy, busy days, Mother took snatches of time to teach us eternal truths…and those truths took root and continue to bear fruit.

Mother was not and is not perfect—she'd want you to know that. But she is the most biblically beautiful woman I know. What a privilege to conclude this study by rising up and calling her blessed, and by encouraging you, my precious sister in Christ, to follow in her biblically beautiful footsteps. P.S. Want to learn more about biblical beauty? Read some of the books on my recommended book list (you'll find it on the following pages). I think you'll love 'em!

Week Six • *Becoming an Ideal Woman*

An Ideal Woman in the making is <u>*becoming*</u>:

1. A _____, valuable help to others. *Prov. 31:11–12*

2. A _____-_____ and a hard worker. *Prov. 31:13, 17, 19, 27*

3. A skilled _____ and servant to her family.
    Prov. 31:14–15, 21–23

4. An organized _____ and overseer. *Prov. 31:15, 21, 27*

5. A wise _____ and good steward. *Prov. 31:16, 18*

6. A gracious _____ to those in need. *Prov. 31:20*

7. An excellent _____. *Prov. 31:16, 24*

8. A strong, dignified, _____ woman. *Prov. 31:21, 25*

9. A wise, kind _____, educator, and encourager. *Prov. 31:26*

What's her secret? How can she do all this? Answer: Because she is…

10. A woman who _____ God and gives Him priority.
    Prov. 31:30

NOTES:

Week One

[1] contentious. Dictionary.com. *Dictionary.com Unabridged*. Random House, Inc. http://dictionary.reference.com/browse/contentious (accessed: June 02, 2010).

[2] reverence. Dictionary.com. *Dictionary.com Unabridged*. Random House, Inc. http://dictionary.reference.com/browse/reverence (accessed: June 11, 2010).

Week Three

[3] Warren Baker, Eugene Carpenter, *The Complete Word Study Dictionary Old Testament* (Chattanooga, TN: AMG Publishers, 2003), 405.

[4] Ibid.

Week Four

[5] contentious. Dictionary.com. *Dictionary.com Unabridged*. Random House, Inc. http://dictionary.reference.com/browse/contentious (accessed: June 02, 2010).

[6] Spiros Zodhiates, *The Complete Word Study Dictionary New Testament* (Chattanooga, TN: AMG Publishers, 1993), 62.

[7] Ibid, 1031.

[8] Ibid, 1469.

[9] Ibid.

[10] Annie Chapman, *The Mother-in-Law Dance: Can Two Women Love the Same Man and Still Get Along?* (Eugene, Oregon: Harvest House Publishers, 2004), 37.

Week Six

[11] Warren Baker, *The Complete Word Study Dictionary Old Testament* (Chattanooga, TN: AMG Publishers, 2003), 334.

RECOMMENDED BOOKS:

Ruth: A Portrait, The Story of Ruth Bell Graham
By Patricia Cornwell
Doubleday

Teen Virtue 2: A Teen Girl's Guide to Relationships
By Vicki Courtney
Broadman & Holman Publishers

Lies Young Women Believe and the Truth That Sets Them Free
By Nancy Leigh DeMoss
Moody Publishers

For Young Women Only: What You Need to Know About How Guys Think
By Shaunti Feldhahn and Lisa a. Rice
Multnomah Books

A Lineage of Grace
By Francine Rivers
Tyndale House

Big Girls Don't Whine
By Jan Silvious
W Publishing Group

Smart Girls Think Twice
By Jan Silvious
Thomas Nelson

Shop Priority

Visit Priority's online store to find out more about Bible studies, DVDs, and CDs by Laurie Cole. Each product will encourage and equip you to give God priority.

www.priorityministries.org/shop

Beauty by THE BOOK

Bible Study

Discover the do's and don'ts of Biblical beauty at any age in this practical 7-week study from Proverbs.

There is a Season

Bible Study

An 11-week study for women, designed to help you experience contentment in every season of life.

The Temple

Bible Study

Priority's *"you glo, girl"* 11-week Bible study will help you discover how to *glo*–glorify God.

Audio CD sets

Resources available for these studies: Workbooks, Small Group CD-ROM Leader Guides, Video Lectures, and Audio Lectures.

Monthly Newsletter

Priority Ministries' monthly e-newsletter, is our opportunity to *glo*–to give God glory–as Laurie Cole and the Priority staff share the latest scoop about Priority Ministries. Visit us online to ***subscribe*** or read the latest issue.

www.priorityministries.org/glogirl

Connect with Priority

Priority Partners

Priority Partners believe in the mission of Priority Ministries and support it with their generous financial gifts. Would you prayerfully consider becoming a Partner and helping us reach and teach women to love God most and seek Him first?

Become a monthly or one-time donor. Either way, your financial gifts provide vital support for this ministry! For more information about becoming a Priority Partner, visit our website:

www.priorityministries.org/support

Priority *Sorority*

Priority Sorority is an online bulletin board where you can post your praise to God for the way He is working in your life, or read what others are saying about a Priority Bible Study. So, c'mon...join today! Become a Priority Sorority Sister!

- Share your testimony.
- Read other testimonies.
- Be encouraged!

www.priorityministries.org

Priority Ministries

Encouraging Women to Give God Glory & Priority

www.priorityministries.org

Made in the USA
Charleston, SC
24 January 2013